Praise for

Blue Like Play Dough

"I couldn't put *Blue Like Play Dough* down. Tricia's love of God comes through on every page as she shows what motherhood is like when God wields His rolling pin and smoothes the rough edges of her life. Before you know it, your heart will be putty in God's hands, too."

—GINGER KOLBABA, editor, *Today's Christian Woman*

"With fresh, disarming honesty, Tricia Goyer gives us a glimpse into the challenges of motherhood and womanhood as we know it oh-so-well. She then gently nudges us to remain pliable in the hands of the One who is deliberate in His plans for us. A surrendered life is a beautiful life. Thanks, Tricia, for giving us an authentic picture of what that sort of life looks like."

—ROBIN JONES GUNN, best-selling author of the Christy Miller series and the Sisterchicks series

"A hopeful book that moms will relish, *Blue Like Play Dough* is an honest, peel-back-the-covers look at the creative way God shapes us through childhood and parenthood. Tricia Goyer explores her own weaknesses along the journey, revealing her desire to serve the God who forms strength and joy and perseverance within her. A compelling, fresh read."

—Mary E. DeMuth, author of *Authentic Parenting in a Postmodern Culture*

"I didn't even know I needed to read this book until I found myself weeping as Tricia's story reached right into my mothering heart. Part memoir and part self-help, *Blue Like Play Dough* is a must read for every mother who has ever doubted her purpose. An honest, hopeful read that will hearten moms no matter what stage of motherhood they are in."

—TINA ANN FORKNER, author of *Ruby Among Us* and *Rose House*

"Tricia's story reveals a great truth: that as God uses us to grow our kids, He grows us in the process too."

—MARY BYERS, author of *Making Work at Home Work* and *The Mother Load*

"The best hostesses make you feel welcome in their home, a part of the family. Likewise, the best authors make you feel welcome as you visit them in the pages of their books. Tricia Goyer does that in *Blue Like Play Dough* as she invites you to come into her life and hang out with her family, and she doesn't apologize for the messiness of family life. Instead, with refreshing vulnerability and transparency, she shows us all that it's okay to be imperfect in the hands of a God whose love for His own is perfect."

—NANCY KENNEDY, author of *Girl on a Swing* and *Lipstick Grace*

"Tricia's book is a masterpiece on motherhood—sculpted by her hands—shaped by her love for God."

—MARGARET MCSWEENEY, author of *Pearl Girls: Encountering Grit, Experiencing Grace*

"*Blue Like Play Dough* had me nodding, laughing, crying, dog-earing favorite pages, and saying, 'Wow, I'm not the only mom who feels that way? I'm not weird?' Honest, gut-wrenching, and funny—this is the kind of book every mom needs to read and keep on her shelf—like a longtime friend—there to walk beside you, drink coffee with you, encourage you. Loved this book!"

—KIMBERLEY WOODHOUSE, author of *Welcome Home: Our Family's Journey to Extreme Joy*

Blue
Like Play
Dough

the **shape** of **motherhood**
in the **grip** of **God**

TRICIA **GOYER**

MULTNOMAH
B O O K S

BLUE LIKE PLAY DOUGH
PUBLISHED BY MULTNOMAH BOOKS
12265 Oracle Boulevard, Suite 200
Colorado Springs, Colorado 80921

All Scripture quotations, unless otherwise indicated, are taken from the Holy
Bible, New International Version®. NIV®. Copyright © 1973, 1978, 1984
by International Bible Society. Used by permission of Zondervan Publishing
House. All rights reserved. Scripture quotations marked (MSG) are taken from
The Message by Eugene H. Peterson. Copyright © 1993, 1994, 1995, 1996,
2000, 2001, 2002. Used by permission of NavPress Publishing Group. All
rights reserved.

Details in some anecdotes and stories have been changed to protect the identities
of the persons involved.

ISBN 978-1-60142-152-4

ISBN 978-1-60142-177-7 (electronic)

Published in the United States by WaterBrook Multnomah, an imprint of the
Crown Publishing Group, a division of Random House Inc., New York.

MULTNOMAH and its mountain colophon are registered trademarks of Random
House Inc.

Library of Congress Cataloging-in-Publication Data
Goyer, Tricia.
    Blue like play dough : the shape of motherhood in the grip of God / Tricia
Goyer.—1st ed.
        p. cm.
    ISBN 978-1-60142-152-4—ISBN 978-1-60142-177-7 (electronic)
    1. Mothers—Religious life. 2. Motherhood—Religious aspects—Christianity.
I. Title.
    BV4529.18.G685 2009
    248.8'431—dc22

                                2009001296

 Printed in the United States of America

2009—First Edition

10 9 8 7 6 5 4 3 2 1

SPECIAL SALES
Most WaterBrook Multnomah books are available at special quantity discounts
when purchased in bulk by corporations, organizations, and special-interest
groups. Custom imprinting or excerpting can also be done to fit special needs.
For information, please e-mail SpecialMarkets@WaterBrookMultnomah.com or
call 1-800-603-7051.

To John
My life partner and true love. Thank you for walking with me as I'm squished and stretched…and for letting me write about the mess of it!

Contents

Foreword

As much as I care about having a Mary Heart in a Martha World, I'm coming to realize that another important adventure begins for women when we choose to have a Play Dough Heart in a Lego World! Something wonderful happens when we choose to surrender our ideas of how things must be and instead allow God to shape us. Then the Holy Spirit can take our willingness and make something infinitely more beautiful than all our carefully constructed plans could have ever accomplished.

This book and Tricia Goyer's life are proof of that.

I'll never forget the day I first met Tricia. As a beginning writer, I was excited to meet someone further down the road than I, not to mention one who had let me know she was willing to help me on my journey. At her home, we laughed as we chattered over a cup of tea about the ins and outs of publishing. But I have to confess I felt a little intimidated. Tricia's house was in pristine order, her kids well behaved, her office an organizer's dream. In short, she appeared to be everything I was not. The fact she was ten years younger didn't help. But Tricia's sweet authenticity and genuine acceptance overcame my insecurities. One cup of tea and we became fast friends.

As impressed as I was with the twenty-something Tricia I met fourteen years ago, I can honestly say my admiration for her has only grown. Oh, her house isn't nearly as clean now, and her office…well, let's just say the piles of research and books do my little heart good. But the beauty of my friend's life now is absolutely breathtaking! Rather than focusing on shaping a perfectly ordered life, she has chosen to be moldable clay in God's hands. Tricia is still everything she was, but she has become so much more.

I'm privileged to recommend *Blue Like Play Dough* for your personal reading. You will be both charmed and challenged by Tricia's wonderful book. I've laughed and cried through its pages. Most of all, I've experienced a renewed desire to surrender all that I am into my Father's trustworthy hands. After all, He has a much better idea of what He "had in mind when He made the original me," as Charlie Shedd wrote.

Though we may all tremble a bit at the thought, I pray we each come to that sweet point of surrender. For us it will be an incredibly freeing and transforming act of becoming…play dough in God's hands.

—JOANNA WEAVER, author of *Having a Mary Heart in a Martha World* and *Having a Mary Spirit*

Prologue

Before I knew play dough could be bought in the store, I remember playing with salt dough my mom had made. It was warm in my hands and it smelled yeasty, like the bakery downtown. I squished it and formed it into a tiny baby with chubby arms and legs. I loved dolls, and I loved imagining what it would be like when I would be a mom. Someday I'd have a baby of my own instead of a salt-dough creation.

But when I had kids, I felt like I was the one being squished and pressed. At times I felt like I was being poked as I tried to deal with the 101 needs of my kids. I felt stretched as I struggled through things I'd hoped I'd never have to face—like hospitalized children, disobedient children, lost children (more than once on all counts). I felt pulled when I tried to balance raising kids, taking care of our house, serving in church, and following my dreams. There were even days when I felt as if I was literally being pounded—by life, by my hang-ups, by my own insecurities and doubts that I was "good enough" as a mom.

One day I was praying about all the hard stuff in life, and into my mind came an image of a blue lump of play dough. As I focused on it, I realized the lump wasn't something my kids or I held in our hands. Rather it was something God held in His. I was that lump. As I watched God pull and tug, I saw that He was following a pattern. He had something in mind. God, the artist, was shaping me, forming me to represent an image of His Son.

The image was there, and then it was gone. Donald Miller had blue jazz. I had blue play dough. I tried not to be disappointed.

In each of our lives, there is molding and shaping to be done. Perhaps I needed more work than most, but as I look back on my life, I realize that if there is one thing that all the stretching and poking and smashing has taught me, it's that I never want to be anywhere but in the grip of God.

I still often ask Him to rescue me from the pressures that come with being a mom. For the most part, He doesn't. Instead, if I'm willing, He uses them to change me on the inside. In His hands I'm being transformed, one squeeze at a time.

Chapter 1

In the Middle of My Mess

I never thought I could meet God here. In my home. In my mess. In the midst of my ordinary suburban life. To me, God was someone you met at church or connected with at weekly Bible study. I knew deep down it was possible to have mountaintop moments, but I believed they came during weeklong spiritual retreats, hourlong morning Quiet Times, and a once-a-year women's conference.

Instead, I found God in surprising places. I found Him as I sat on the couch cuddling with my three-year-old and reading *Goodnight Moon* for the 2,345th time. He spoke to me as I made dinner and even as I stuffed laundry into rickety dresser drawers. I heard Him in the midst of my untidy, desperately-in-need-of-a-reorg life. I found God, experienced Him…well…while mixing Kool-Aid and playing with play dough.

And it's a good thing God allowed Himself to be found there, because as a mom my opportunities for solitude, contemplation, and three hymns and a prayer are few and far between.

I used to think the ones who knew God best were nuns and monks who lived high in the hills. I imagined it must be hard for such people to separate themselves and to give up so much. What they had, I believed, was true devotion and an ultimate connection with God. Everyone else—those of us who lived ordinary lives—missed out. Well, I don't think that anymore.

Yes, I still think nuns and monks are devoted people, but in a way they have it easy. They find God in routines and rituals. They talk to God because there is no one else around. They don't have to deal with bad drivers cutting them off and then flipping them off. Or with grass stains on a *new* pair of capris that actually fit and don't make their butts look too big. Or with a child practicing her name one hundred times on the bathroom floor in permanent marker. Sure, their prayers sound eloquent, but a mom's prayers for a sick baby are just as pious and maybe more passionate.

In my way of thinking, the most devoted people are moms who whisper prayers for their neighbor, their friend, and their brother (who's messing up yet again) while watching their kids play in the sandbox. Moms who try to read their Bibles while *Dora the Explorer* is blaring on the TV in the next room. Moms who stop to talk with an elderly man at the grocery store about the creamed corn, not because they even like creamed corn, but because they want to show a lonely person the love of Jesus.

I think God would agree. I believe He sees the challenges and the effort. He appreciates the smallest turning of our attention to Him or to others for Him.

Even though seeking God is worthy, that doesn't mean it's easy or natural. In fact, it almost seems wrong to squeeze God into the middle of a busy, ordinary life. God is BIG. My pursuits are small. God is GLORIOUS. Scrubbing sinks and changing poopy diapers is not. Nor is pushing a shopping cart filled with teetering toiletries, humming "Girls Just Want to Have Fun" as the song plays through the store speakers.

I've read many books written by people who "went away with God." The authors often write about how God speaks to people in solitary, beautiful places. But not all the places He visits are beautiful. Or solitary. My life is proof of that.

Truth be told, it wasn't *I* who discovered *God*. He came down and met me where I was. It doesn't matter to Him that I can hardly see my desk under the piles of mail and bills and kids' craft projects. He doesn't care that I'm twenty pounds overweight (or maybe thirty, no matter what my driver's license says). He loves me just as I am. He knows my to-do list and that I'll never get to the end of it. Ever. God sees my heart. He understands that I'm trying to get my life in order so I can focus on family dinners and Bible reading times. He knows I'm working at not feeling envious that my neighbor is thinner than I am and has a better flower garden. My flaws neither surprise Him nor dissuade Him from entering my life.

It's not as if God says, "I was going to visit you today, but I think I'll wait until you balance that checkbook, clean out your fridge, and start that Bible study you've been meaning to get around to." God's not like that. He walked with dirty, smelly shepherds and hung out with jailed prophets, so I don't think my waist-high laundry pile is going to scare Him off.

Still, I struggle with feeling as if I have to clean up before I approach God. Organize my closets. Transform my kids. Rearrange my priorities. Renew my heart. I forget that God wants me just as I am. That belonging to Him is enough.

Like the prodigal son in Luke 15:11–32, I need to remember who my Father is. The kid had it all, and he threw it away. He was broke. He was hungry. He was dirty. He was a mess. Then he remembered his father and his home.

For the prodigal son, it wasn't just about going back to his home. It was also about letting his dad take care of him. I need to do the same. And if I took two minutes to think about it— as I'm doing now—I'd realize the perfection I long for will never be found in the place I live and parent and strive. It's found in who I turn to. In who is waiting for me with open arms.

The problem isn't whether God will show up. It's all about me not being aware that God is *already* here…that He has been in my life all along. And that He doesn't care about my mess. Sometimes I do better at remembering. And other times, well…

I live in a house with my husband, my grandma, my three teens, and a foreign exchange student we invited into our home just so we could make sure life didn't get too boring. That's seven people, each involved in numerous activities, each with his or her own schedule. Circles and scribbles and arrows fill my desk calendar. White spaces are few and far between. Daily life keeps me running. Add in volunteering at church and my work projects, and I wonder if it's possible to think, let alone contemplate.

While I'm no longer potty training and all my kids have learned to write and read and say please and thank you, I've discovered that every season comes with challenges of its own. Right now I'm in a season where little messes sprout up around me like dandelions on a manicured lawn. As soon as I try to cut one down, the seeds scatter and weeds sprout up in a dozen more places.

In the last two months, my nineteen-year-old son, Cory, had two knee surgeries (due to basketball injuries). And my daughter, Leslie, celebrated her sixteenth birthday with a "Never Been Kissed Party," which means that my years of lectures about abstinence and purity have paid off thus far. My youngest son, Nathan, has been helping me housebreak a dog that, for the past year, has assumed the downstairs bathroom was his potty spot too.

I used to think stumbling over LEGO blocks was irritating. Now I live with a teen driver, a social butterfly, and a child who must believe that showers spray acid, judging by the lengths he goes to avoid them. On a daily basis, I'm not sure who is going where with whom…or if any of my kids are clean enough to be going out at all!

When I read the familiar Scripture verse, "Be still, and know that I am God," my stomach knots and my thoughts bounce around like a Ping-Pong ball on steroids. Even as I try to focus on the words, my mind wanders to the phone calls I need to return. I find myself trying to stack and restack the piles in order to make them seem more appealing and not quite so overwhelming.

Yet I know this verse doesn't necessarily mean I have to still my body in order to connect with God. In the middle of my busy life, I can refocus my thoughts and my mind and my heart on Him. I can be fixed on God, even when my feet are hustling. I can look for Him, listen for Him, even if the looking and listening happen in the short drive I take to pick my daughter up from her job at a fast-food restaurant. Or in the prayers I offer up as I shave my legs in the shower.

Being still is trusting that when I do fill the white space with some quiet moments (which I try to do daily), God will have something better in store for me and my kids than what I could've come up with on my own. (Like the afternoon when, instead of cleaning off my desk, I took my daughter for coffee. That inner urging led to great conversation about issues I didn't realize Leslie was dealing with.)

Being still is realizing that even though the world is traveling around me at breakneck speed, sometimes—most times—

God's schedule is in the horse-and-buggy mode. Just because life is moving faster and my needs are growing like kernels of popcorn in the microwave, it doesn't mean that God *has to* answer my urgent prayers in the next .287 seconds. In fact, sometimes I think He holds off on purpose, because the greater my need, the more I seek Him. In the end the seeking and waiting and trusting may be more important than the answer.

The mess isn't going to get cleaned up today, but that doesn't mean I need to hold God at bay. He loves joining me, even if I'm placing Him into my chaos. In fact, if God had His way, I'm sure He'd write Himself into all parts of my life, using permanent marker, reminding me of where He wants to be—everywhere. In all of my life. And if I close my eyes, I can see His message in my day, in my life:

Insert God here.

Chapter 2

Some Things Stick

A s a mom I take care of the groceries and the mail, and I make snacks for the youth group get-together. I take care of the library books, the bills, the toilets, and coupons for one dollar off any box of cereal. I run permission slips up to the church two minutes before the scheduled outing, and I hustle kids around for shoe shopping, swimsuit shopping, and deodorant buying, because I—of course—hold the checkbook. If there is no milk in the fridge, I hear the grumbles.

The problem arises when I face my schedule and my to-do list as if everything is up to me. Self-sufficiency is one of my biggest weaknesses. I handle things because I've always handled them. Maybe it's because I learned at a young age the importance of taking care of myself. Of finding my own path, my own way.

It's weird how some things stick in our minds from our younger years, and other, important things—like the first time we tied our shoes or the first day of kindergarten—don't occupy a blip of memory. I've learned that if I look back at the events, which play through my mind like a movie, I can sometimes see what those key moments taught me and how they molded me, even though I didn't understand how I was being formed at the time.

———

I don't know why Mom couldn't take me. Maybe she had to go to work or was off to do something with her friends, or maybe she had to take care of my baby brother. Instead, my new dad drove me to the birthday party. He'd married my mom the previous year, and I still didn't know much about him. Didn't want to.

"It's at the day care south of town," my mom told Ron before we left. "Do you know where that is? By the apartments?"

"Yes, I know where that is," he responded.

I held the present in my lap as we drove. We passed my aunt's house and then the turnoff that would take me to my grandma's house. A few minutes later, we stopped at a yellow house with big yellow apartments behind it. I climbed out of the car, and my new dad drove away.

I didn't see any other kids. I didn't see anyone for that matter. I cautiously walked up to the front door and knocked. A woman answered. Behind her a man sat on a couch. He peered around her to look at me.

"Can I help you?" the woman asked.

"I came for the birthday party." I hugged the package close to my chest.

"I'm sorry, there's no birthday party here. You have the wrong house." She looked behind me, most likely looking for a car or a parent.

"Come inside. Do you know your phone number? Should we call someone?"

The man rose from the couch and stood beside her. I'd never seen these people before. My stomach hurt.

"No. I'm going to my aunt's house." I turned and hurried away.

I knew in what direction my aunt lived. It wasn't too far away, just down the road.

"I can drive you," the woman called after me. I ignored her and walked down the sidewalk to the road, half walking, half jogging, hurrying away as fast as my legs would carry me. Cars zoomed by. I held the present tighter as I scurried on.

I thought my aunt's house was nearby, but I couldn't see it from where I was. The road stretched on before me. I forgot about the party. I still held the present, but I didn't care about it anymore. I just wanted to be in a safe place.

My chin trembled, but I set it determinedly. A car pulled up beside me. It was the woman from the house. She called out, "Where are you going? Get in. I'll give you a ride."

I knew better than to get in and just ignored her.

Soon the houses started to look familiar. Up ahead I saw one close to my aunt's house. It had gray shingles set in a zigzag pattern. It always made me think of large, silver gum wrappers plastered on the outer walls.

I stopped at a busy street, looked both ways, and crossed. Within a few minutes I hurried up the steep driveway to my aunt's house and ran inside without knocking. My Aunt Jeanette looked at me, surprised.

My mom picked me up later and gave me a big hug. My feet hurt, and I didn't feel like going to a party. She took me there anyway. All eyes turned and stared as I entered. I wanted to turn and hide. They urged me to come and join their game. I refused.

The other kids were just finishing their cake. The presents had already been opened. I'd missed it all.

I sat in a little chair and watched the others from a distance. I'd found my way to safety this time, but what if another time I was too far away? I knew I never wanted anything like that to happen again. Others couldn't be trusted. I would take care of myself. I could trust myself.

I was only five, but I took the lesson to heart.

I got really good at taking care of myself. In the second grade I started getting myself up, getting dressed, fixing my own breakfast, and then catching the bus.

In the third grade, I'd walk my brother home from the school on top of the hill, down the walking trail, over the tracks, and across busy Main Street. I'd help myself with homework, and I'd dream about my future family. A family I could take care of like I wanted to be taken care of.

Growing up, I was used to making my own plans, finding my own way, depending on my own resources. So it was only natural that as a teenager I tried to fill my needs for love and attention by turning to guys. I grabbed whatever I wanted and thought I needed. My relationships were influenced by how cute a guy was, how cute he thought I was, and the level of warm fuzzies I felt when we were together. I was certain I'd find the perfect guy, date all through school, and then have a Cinderella wedding when we were old enough to tie the knot.

I used to lie in bed at night, thinking about the first time I'd tell my future husband (who would be completely wonderful, of course) that I was expecting. My imagined hubby would come home from a long day at work to a white house with green shutters. I'd have a candlelight dinner waiting. I even knew what I'd serve: baby back ribs, baby carrots, and baby peas.

I would be glowing—not from the candlelight, but from the joy of expectancy. My husband would glance up at me from across the table and cock one eyebrow. I would nod enthusiastically. We'd embrace, and then we'd head to JCPenney to pick out our first baby outfit! It would be perfect.

But my life didn't follow the fairy tale. Far from it.

It didn't happen that way the first time I got pregnant. Or the second.

The second time, I was a college-bound senior, on the year-book staff, and a cheerleader. It no longer mattered that my boyfriend was cute or that he thought I was cute or that he gave me warm fuzzies. Warm fuzzies don't last through the hard stuff.

Our relationship ended when my boyfriend insisted I have an abortion, as I'd done at his urging the first time I got pregnant. Still feeling the pain of that decision, I refused. I was determined to have this baby, no matter what anyone said, no matter the looks of disapproval I received.

I wore my shame like a chain-mail cloak. And it was a heavy cloak indeed. Maybe it was so heavy because, in the back of my mind where I'd hidden my childhood faith, I believed there was a God who knew everything, saw everything, including how I'd been living.

I grew up in church. There were moments when I believed God, moments when I loved Him. But after my unplanned pregnancies, I didn't know what to think of God or what to think about what He thought of me. Instead, my plan was to take care of myself and my baby.

I didn't feel beautiful anymore. I didn't feel worthy, but God paid that no mind. I ran, but God followed me.

Before I discovered that God could come down in the mess of motherhood, I, like David in the Bible, learned that He could come down in the mess of a broken heart and a fractured life.

David is one of the most popular Bible figures. One could even call him infamous. Like me, he went through a time when he tried to take care of things himself.

David the shepherd turned to God and defeated a giant, but David the king wanted a beautiful woman named Bathsheba and took the matter into his own hands. Two huge problems. Only one led to David's victory—the giant one he submitted to God. The one he handled himself led to an affair, a murder, grief over a lost child, and brokenness. And when he'd completely messed things up, David turned to God to fix them up.

So did I. When I got the family I wanted before I was ready, I had nowhere to turn *but* to God. Seventeen years old and pregnant, I found God. And, I realized, He'd been waiting for me to find Him for a very long time.

When I was five, trying to find my way to my aunt's house, God was by my side. When I dreamed of my future family, God knew I would take the wrong path getting there, yet He was patient. He knew there would be the right moment when I'd come to the end of myself.

When my kids were small, they'd often whine about their untied shoes or fuss about their inability to get the pieces of their craft project to glue just so. But instead of jumping in, I'd watch and listen and wait, even as their complaints escalated and their attempts failed time and time again. Why? Because I liked to see them struggle? No, I waited because I wanted them to seek me out and to know that I could help them *if* they asked. I wanted to be someone they could turn to as a first choice, not as a last option.

My kids are finally starting to understand this concept. A few weeks ago Cory was working on a video project, and he asked me for input. And Leslie and Nathan have both recently turned to me for advice about friends.

I'm learning too. Some days I still try to tackle things on my own. I attempt to merge my to-do list with my kids' lives, urging them to help around the house through pleas and charts and threats. I'm quick to tell them how things need to happen, but I'm slow to listen. I snap when I'm tired and cry when I'm overwhelmed. But there are more days when I remember God is by my side.

I don't have to find my way alone. Not only is God with me, but He can be trusted to provide the protection, love, and answers I need every step of this parenting journey.

It's not all up to me, after all.

Chapter 3

I'll Alter Him

"Hey Dad, Mom and I came up with a great idea for next summer," Cory spoke from the backseat of our SUV, leaning forward to talk over his dad's shoulder.

As soon as the words were out of Cory's mouth, my stomach tightened and I knew trouble lay just ahead. I'd meant to talk to John about my conversation with Cory, but then I forgot all about it. Now, I had a sinking feeling that John's response wasn't going to be as positive as Cory had planned.

"Yeah, what's that?" John glanced over at me with an uplifted eyebrow. I forced a smile.

"Mom said that she'd pay for me to attend screenwriting school next summer in Hollywood, and in exchange I'll write a screenplay for one of her novels."

"Oh, she did, did she?" I could tell from John's voice that there were multiple layers of meaning to his sentence. First, John was wondering about the cost. Screenwriting school wasn't the same as summer camp. Second, I knew he thought I made things too easy on the kids, which was mostly true. I loved the idea of having a screenwriter in the family, and I wanted it to work. I wanted to help Cory succeed, and it seemed like a good way. And third, and most importantly, John was aggravated that I had talked about this idea with Cory without even mentioning it to him. You'd think something like spending thousands of dollars and sending our son to Hollywood for three months would merit conversation with my husband. But when it comes down to it, it has always been much easier for me to decide these things and worry about the consequences later.

This is something I've struggled with throughout our marriage. I'm a spur-of-the-moment, "that sounds great" type of girl. John has always been more thoughtful. Okay, scratch that. John actually *thinks* things through. He weighs different options. He considers the various outcomes.

"But don't you think it's a great idea?" The words spilled out, yet my eyes were focused on the roadway ahead of us rather than on John. "Maybe Cory can even pitch the screenplay to producers, and then they will make a movie. The teachers in this program actually work in the industry, you know."

John again glanced at me, but I could see his hands tightening around the steering wheel. "This is something we need to talk about." His voice was stern, his words laced with anger. I knew I'd brought this on myself. If I had my way, I'd make many more decisions without consulting John. I like throwing caution to the wind, spending money, and dreaming big with hopes that things *will* turn out all right in the end. I like my independence. I like things my way…and then I wonder why my kids have a problem with obedience! (Wow, I wonder where they got that self-reliant attitude from?)

Not that I feel I have to obey John. He's not a dictator, and I don't run around following his every command. Rather, I need to include him—in conversations, in dreams, in ideas, and in plans. I need to remember that we're in this together. After all, the one who is closest to me (my husband) should most likely have an influence on which path I'm running toward.

———

I have to admit that I thought more about John becoming my husband than John becoming Cory's dad. We got married when Cory was nine months old, but we'd been dating since Cory was two weeks old, so I didn't think there would be much transition. I was wrong.

I was Cory's main caregiver, so I figured I knew best how to hold him, feed him, discipline him, and interact with him. I wrestled with the same thing after having Leslie and Nathan. I also believed our problem of butting heads over our dealings with the kids would only be resolved when John changed and started doing things *my* way.

It wasn't like we were having big arguments or daily discussions. It was just little stuff that we had opposite views on. Stuff that bugged me, like how John held one-year-old Cory by the back of his sleeper pajamas and zoomed him around the room. It seemed a little rough. During Leslie's toddler years, I didn't appreciate how John insisted on ignoring her tantrums. Didn't he see that she was little and just needed to be held? coddled? Or when he would flip Nathan upside down and swing him around by his feet. It was, again, just too rough in my opinion. Nathan was a toddler, not a toy. And then there was the way John disciplined. His voice was too harsh, and he didn't seem to understand that kids are kids. I thought he demanded too much obedience too soon.

But looking back, I can see that the main problem wasn't that John didn't listen to my opinion of how things should be handled. The main problem was that I thought I knew the *only* way. Maybe it's because I knew what I loved most as a kid. When I parented, I remembered times when I felt loved and appreciated by my family members. And I wanted to re-create that environment for my kids.

———

Warmth radiated from the wood stove in the corner of the double-wide mobile home. The pillow under my head smelled like flowers. Or maybe peaches. I listened to female voices coming from my grandma's kitchen. My mom and grandma worked side by side, cleaning up after lunch. In the TV room, noise from the football game blared from the television. The announcer's voice was far too loud. It was quieter in the room I'd escaped to. I liked it better. The stuff was fancier in here, and there was no television. It was my favorite spot to escape to and pretend to sleep.

I curled to my side and pulled the throw blanket tight to my chin, trying to ignore the noisy complaints of my dad as he mumbled about the bad call made by the refs against the 49ers. My brother, Ronnie, was only in first grade, but he booed with him.

Ronnie was my dad's real son, and although everyone pretended Ron was my dad, I knew the truth. I felt the difference. Until a year ago, I had a different last name—my grandparents' last name. But deeper than that, I noticed Ron liked spending time with my brother more than with me. He talked to me mostly when I did something wrong—then I really heard about it.

If I could just get things right, then maybe he'd be proud of me. And maybe if my real dad found me, he'd approve of me even when I messed up, just like Ron did with Ronnie.

I heard the water shut off in the kitchen, and I guessed my mom and grandma were done with the dishes. I slowed my breathing and tried not to move a muscle. I didn't want to leave. Maybe if I fell asleep I could stay. I felt safe at my grandma and grandpa's house. Appreciated. It was the place I liked best.

Our home didn't have the same feel as my grandparents' house. We lived in a rental—the most recent of many. We seemed to move to a different house every year, and though each one looked different, they all felt the same—cold, empty. Walking into my grandma's house was like walking into a warm hug.

I felt happy as I listened to the sound of the dishes being put away and the cupboards closing. I tried harder to pretend to sleep. Footsteps neared, and I felt the presence of someone standing beside the couch.

"Tricia. Time to wake up. We need to go home." My mom stirred me, with her hand on my arm, but I didn't budge.

"Linda, let her be. She's tired. We can take her home later." It was my grandma's voice. My grandma was always on my side. I was always "in" with her.

I tried to hide my face. If I smiled, I would ruin everything.

"No, Mom, I won't have you going out in this weather. Tricia can come home with us. If she's tired, she can sleep in her own bed."

I heard the TV clicking off and my dad's and little brother's voices. My brother was mad about something. Maybe the 49ers didn't win. He was always mad about something.

"Well, at least have Ron carry her to the car," my grandma insisted.

"She's too heavy. She can walk." My mom shook my shoulder again.

I gave up pretending.

My eyes fluttered open, slowly. I yawned and stretched.

"Time to go home," my mom said.

I knew better than to argue. Arguing never worked.

Without a word, I put my coat on, then I turned to say good-bye to my grandparents. "Love you, sweetheart." My grandma placed both hands on my cheeks, and she gave me a soft peck on my nose. They weren't just words. They were more. I could feel her love in her touch. I could see the truth of her words in her gaze.

We headed outside. The icy cold wind struck my face. It was always windy in Weed. That's how the town started, after all. Some guy named Abner Weed tried to find a windy place to build a sawmill. The wind, we'd been told, dried the wood. All I knew was that it nearly blew me over on bad days.

I climbed in the back of the freezing car and shivered, knowing only a cold bedroom awaited me.

Why couldn't I have just stayed in the warmth?

My happiest childhood memories involved being cared for and coddled by my grandparents. They spoke to me in soft voices. They never disciplined me. They were gentle. They fed me good food and treated me to special presents. What I didn't understand (but John did) is that while it's okay for grandparents to act that way, it's not a good parenting model. Kids need discipline. They need structure. They need parents to raise their voices…especially in times of danger. They need to know when wrong is wrong. Coddled kids become narcissistic adults. Adults who think only of themselves and not others.

John also knew better than I did what boys needed. The more he shared some of his favorite childhood memories, the better I understood that they didn't involve being cuddled on the couch. Sure he enjoyed hugs and stuff from his mom, but John's best memories of his dad were times when they interacted roughly. When he was thrown into the air or chased around the yard. When he was tackled and tickled. From John, I learned that, while girls understand they're loved from hugs and kisses, boys understand this when they're wrangled and wrestled. Who would have thought?!

In my home when I was growing up, discipline and punishment were the same thing. They were yelling and slaps on the arm. They were deeds done out of anger. I got away with things often, and then I paid for the same offenses when my dad happened to be in a bad mood. Because I didn't understand loving discipline, I was ready to toss it out completely, and yet John (and various parenting books) helped me to understand that boundaries are set up to protect, not to hurt. They also helped me understand that if there aren't consequences for overstepping boundaries, then steps of small sin will lead to leaps toward larger ones. God says the same thing in His Word.

Only irresponsible parents leave children to fend for themselves. Would you prefer an irresponsible God? We respect our own parents for training and not spoiling us, so why not embrace God's training so we can truly live? While we were children, our parents did what seemed best to them. But God is doing what is best for us, training us to live God's holy best. At the time, discipline isn't much fun. It always feels like it's going against the grain. Later, of course, it pays off handsomely, for it's the well-trained who find themselves mature in their relationship with God. (Hebrews 12:8–11, MSG)

John and I have been married nineteen years now. For the most part, I've stopped trying to figure out how I can alter him—as a father and husband. On our wedding day, I vowed to love, honor, and cherish John. I thought this meant only in the roles of husband and wife. It doesn't. As a mother, I learned I needed to love, honor, and cherish John as a father. To realize that he is the other half of the parenting equation and not just a convenient baby-sitter who is around to give me a break once in a while. It's a part of the molding process that I never expected. Who knew my role as a mother would also help me become a better wife?

No, John's not perfect. I'm not either. But somewhere between his firmness and my tendency toward gentleness and grace, we've found a happy middle. And do you know who's benefiting from our dual molding the most? Our kids. They're seeing glimpses of the two aspects of God in two very fallible people. And personally I think that's exactly the way God designed it.

Chapter 4

If Love Showed Up in Sneakers

The phone rang, and I cringed. I had a feeling who it would be. A family member was going through a lot of struggles. I felt badly for her, but mainly I felt frustrated that I didn't know what to say or do.

Some relationships are easy. They're with people we feel comfortable around. Loved. Then there are other relationships. Ones in which we're always tiptoeing around, hoping we don't step on the other person's toes. This relationship was one of those.

If I answer and say the wrong thing, then she'll get mad at me. I've tried to help before, but nothing has helped.

Maybe I'll say something that will make things worse. Maybe I'll really hurt her feelings. Maybe it's better that I just let the phone ring.

John walked into the kitchen toward the phone.

"Don't answer—" I wasn't able to get the sentence out before he picked it up. Yes, it was her. Yes, she needed to talk.

I rolled my eyes at John and mouthed, "Thanks a lot."

The outside world often comes calling, and sometimes I just want to find a way not to get involved. I do enjoy helping people. I do care, but I almost feel as if each need comes down to "all or nothing." I'll help, and the person will approve of me. I'll fail and ruin everything. I struggle with imagining middle ground. In fact, if I stretch out my arms, I see myself and my ability in my left hand, and I see another's need in my right. In between is a big expanse, with lots of space for me to disappoint.

After all, people call because they want me to *do* something, right? And with each call for help, I have this foreboding that this time I will mess up and fall out of favor. This time I'll lose someone's love for good. Maybe part of my problem is that too often I listen to the nagging, inner voice telling me that not only do I have to *give* the right answer, I have to *be* the answer…for everyone.

I took the phone from John's hands, and I talked with the caller. I tried to listen. I tried to offer help, but I hung up with feelings that it didn't go too well. And as I sat there replaying the conversation in my thoughts, my mind took me back to my good friend…or rather someone who used to be a good friend. She'd had marriage struggles, and I'd offered advice. I prayed for her and with her. I took her to lunch. And when she told me she wanted a divorce, I tried to encourage her to stick it out, to stay in marital counseling a bit longer. I can't forget her angry words as she told me that I just needed to let it go. She was getting a divorce and that was that.

Ever since, I've had this feeling that I could have done more, said more to help her. If I were wiser I could have said something that would have made a difference. But I didn't, and I still feel the tension in our relationship.

I feel a similar tension in my relationship with this family member. No matter what I say, it seems to be the wrong thing. Maybe that's why it's better not to answer these calls for help. I can't mess up—I can't lose out—if I don't get involved.

―

My biggest struggle as a young(er) mom had nothing to do with the kids. Yes, diapers were a pain. Potty training seemed hopeless. And housework was, well, work. But my nemesis was myself.

As long as I can remember, I have looked at life as if I had something to prove. Born to a single mom, I didn't even know my biological father's name growing up. I felt different from everyone else. Incomplete.

In high school, I wanted to "show them." Show them that I could play the role of good girl. Show them I could excel. I only wish I could've put my finger on who "them" was. And when enough *would* be enough.

Things didn't change much after high school. Even though I'd heard a zillion times that God loved me, flaws and all, as a mom I struggled with wanting to please Him and everyone else. Unfortunately most attempts—despite my well-meaning efforts and good intentions—resulted more often in a buzzer than a "ding, ding, ding, you are correct."

I worried that I disciplined my kids too much. Or maybe not enough. That I fed them the wrong foods or allowed their brains to be filled with too much mindless entertainment. I worried I wasn't the helpmate my husband deserved or the friend and church volunteer I ought to be.

Was I focusing on the right things?

Would I look back with regrets on these key developmental years?

What did people see when they looked at me?

I was timid when there was a knock at the door. I dreaded opening the squeaky hinges of our household to allow the outside world in. Was the house clean enough? Were the kids screaming? I wanted people to think well of me (truth be told, I still do!), and I did whatever I could to ensure that they would. If I was asked to do, give, volunteer, help, I had a hard time saying no. *Please love me, accept me, smile…yes, that's right…now, what else do you need?*

I carried around the notion that John was the good guy who married the bad girl. And that, in part, was true. During my high school years, John was in the Marine Corps. On weekends he'd often come home to visit his parents' church, which was the same church my mom attended. On one rare occasion, I, too, went to church. And on that same Sunday—it just so happened—John visited and saw me. He swears that he felt his stomach drop and his face flush. He says he thought I was the most beautiful girl he'd ever seen. After church, he asked his mom about me.

"That's Tricia," Darlyne answered. "Stay away from her. She's trouble."

I laugh every time I retell that story, mostly because Trouble ended up as her daughter-in-law. But for many years I still considered myself that way. As trouble. Trouble to God, who had to rescue me from myself. Trouble to my kids and friends when I couldn't be all they needed. And trouble to John because I wasn't (sigh) the perfect wife.

I moaned as I stepped over a pile of overdue library books and dirty laundry stacked at the top of the stairs and bolted to the bathroom. I threw my hair up in a ponytail and slipped into sweatpants, my mind racing with the two dozen things I needed to accomplish that day: homework to grade, bathrooms to clean, phone calls to return, children to drive around, work deadlines to meet.

Oh, and I needed to clean...and I needed to spend time with my kids. I'd put off playing that board game with them yet again, even though I promised I would.

Tomorrow.

Mixed in with my thoughts were the sounds of two children arguing and a third pleading with me to hurry before she was late for her piano lesson. The dog barked at the UPS truck rumbling by. The phone rang.

Tomorrow I will get everything in order. I'll be a better mom tomorrow.

Then it hit me. As I stood there, hairbrush in one hand and toothbrush in the other, I realized, *This is life.*

Tomorrow wasn't going to be that magical day for me to get it right. *Today* was the day that the memories were made.

As I spent more time in God's Word, the picture I saw there began to reshape how I saw myself. I started to see the Bible as a love story and myself as someone the Creator of the universe was pursuing. More than that, I realized God was in the process at that very moment of creating the happily-ever-after I'd always longed for. One spent with Him in eternity. Forever.

Soon peace began booting those feelings of unworthiness right out the door. Not because I was perfect, but because I was loved.

That was a half dozen years ago, and a few things have changed. Many haven't.

I still haven't been able to keep the house perfect. I never have all my phone calls returned and e-mails answered. Yet since that day, my goal has been to take those "loving thoughts" that God speaks to me in the morning and apply them to my life. Some days I succeed, and other days…well, I fail miserably.

Every day I have to remind myself that I don't have anything to prove. That I can live loved. Because I am.

I'm reminded of this often. If I had wanted love to show up in sneakers and roam around my home, leaving no couch cushion unturned, no sock drawer undisturbed, then I found it in my husband and my three kids.

Even when I burned dinner, when I bounced a check, or when I confessed that my heart and thoughts have not been pure, John's taken my face into his hands and forced me to look into his eyes. "I love you," he says. "I will always love you. Please try to accept that."

It doesn't matter whether I make steaks or hot dogs for dinner, my kids wrap their arms around me and squeeze. They urge me to ignore the floor that's in desperate need of a broom and dustpan and just chill with them. To stop what I'm doing and chat around the kitchen counter or to open our home to their friends on the spur of the moment. They have helped me see that love is making people more important than projects.

I don't get life right 100 percent of the time (or maybe not even 50 percent!), but I know I'm loved—cherished even.

———

There are some people in your life that you have to love (like family members, no matter how much you want to wring their necks). Then there are those you get to love, because for some reason God blessed you by placing them into your life. One of these bonuses to our family is Will.

Will is an amazing young man. He's a youth leader in the youth group that my kids attend. We got to know Will because, as an act of service, he parked cars for the college-age Bible study that was hosted down the street. During wintry nights when Will was filling our driveway with cars, we invited him in and fed him. And in case you don't know what happens when you start to feed a college-age single…he becomes part of your family.

Will likes to hike and hunt, but when he's home he hangs out with us. We don't think much about it. We just enjoy having him here. And because God's been working on this "people not projects" thing with me, it's become more natural to invite others to join our lives without worrying if I'm going to do everything right.

When John and I opened our home to Will, we never expected to get anything in return. We have. Friendship. Thankfulness. In fact, a few months ago I got an e-mail from Will telling us this (in part):

> I like going over to your house, because it is warm and
> quiet and for the food. But the real reason I like going
> over is because of the Love. Your house is just full of it. It
> is strong enough to chase away my insecurities, and there
> is enough to refill me when I feel totally empty. So I
> wanted to tell you thanks for that too.

Will has no idea how I've struggled to connect with God, to feel His love, and to pour it out. He doesn't know how I struggle with trying to help people because of my fear that I'm going to mess things up. It's not like our family made Will a mission; instead, God just expanded our hearts and gave us a tender spot for this wonderful kid, making it natural to open our home. It was simple, really, on our part.

At times I still jump right into work instead of worship, or pretend I have my act together even though I don't. Some days I would rather sit down with a pile of papers to file than relax over coffee. And there are still times I cringe when the phone rings. I cringe when someone needs me. I doubt my own ability to get things right. But I'm learning to remind myself that I'm still a work in progress. So is my life. So are my attempts at showing love.

By physically going to God every morning, I'm placing myself in His hands. His love smoothes out the rough edges and reminds me I don't need to do everything for everyone. I just need to accept love and give it. He'll take care of the rest.

I've been a mom for nineteen years, and I'm still not a perfect parent or person. I'm a mess, actually. But I'm a mess that I let God get a hold of. Not because I'm spiritual, but because I was—and am—desperate. I've done many things wrong, but I do one thing right. When I'm uncertain, I seek God. And I fill up with His love in order to pour it out.

Not always first, but eventually.

Chapter 5

Learning Things Twice and Then Some

I used to have an idea of what homeschooling moms were like—until I became one. While I admired that lifestyle, it was so *not* me.

I'm more likely to drive through Starbucks than to press fresh carrot juice. I watch *Heroes* with my kids and spend more time surfing the Web than weeding an organic garden. (Truth is I've only had one garden in my life, and it was a mess!) Whenever anyone asked me whether I'd be homeschooling our kids, I laughed at the idea.

Then I met Jim and Sandy and their eight kids at church. The oldest was my age and the youngest was Cory's age. What I noticed first was how their teenagers behaved. They enjoyed playing with the younger kids. They enjoyed talking with adults. They liked spending time with their parents. They were respectful and fun to be around. They set themselves apart, not because of how they dressed or how they ate, but because of how they loved.

From the time my kids were toddlers, I'd feared the coming teen years. My kids would throw a tantrum in the middle of the grocery store, and people would respond, "Oh, that's nothing; just wait until they are teens."

I wanted good teens. Caring teens. Teens I could live with!

One day, after I told Sandy how I admired her kids, she told me about homeschooling. After having a front-row seat and noticing the difference in her kids, I wanted to know more about it. Not because I thought spending the next thirteen years of my life teaching my kids would be fun, but because I saw the results, and I was willing to do what I could to get those results for myself.

I pulled a sticker off the workbook sheet and handed it to Cory. It was an image of a pig in tennis shoes. Cory took the sticker, but I could see he was ready for this to be over. He carelessly placed the sticker in the right spot under the word VERBS. I resisted the urge to unpeel it and straighten it. *It's a kindergarten worksheet, for goodness' sake!*

I glanced at the clock. *Four more minutes...* I, too, was ready for our school day to be done.

"Run. *Run* is a verb," I said. "Can you run like this pig?"

Cory jumped up and ran in place. A smile replaced the frown.

"Good job on the running. Can you think of another verb?"

Cory's eyes brightened. He flapped his arms. "Flap!"

"Good job. *Flap* is a verb. *Jump* is a verb, too. Can you jump?"

Cory crouched down low, and then he leapt into the air. "Higher, higher, higher," he chanted.

Nathan and Leslie forgot their toys and jumped to their feet. "Higher, higher, higher," they joined in, although Nathan's words sounded more like "Hi-R. Hi-R."

"*Smile* is a verb too," I grinned.

The kids smiled back.

"So is *laugh*."

The kids laughed.

Nathan, who was two and had no idea what was going on, laughed the hardest.

My eyes met Cory's. "Act out another verb."

He dropped to the floor, curled in a ball, and closed his eyes.

My brow furrowed, and then I got it. "Sleep. Are you sleeping?"

Cory nodded.

"*Sleep* is a verb. Good job." And then, satisfied that I'd managed to mix English with PE, I decided to call it a day.

I wouldn't be honest if I said homeschooling was easy or was always fun, especially in the beginning. I nearly hyperventilated every time I glanced at my five-year-old and thought about the next twelve years. *So much to do, to teach, to get right.*

Not only was I now in charge of my children's physical care and spiritual and moral training, I was also in charge of their education. It was up to me to teach them to read. It was up to me to teach them how to divide and to spell words correctly (yikes!). Yet I quickly learned the cool thing about kids. They live "in the moment." My seven-year-old wasn't concerned about placement for his SATs. He was happy just listening to the Berenstain Bears and all the trouble they get into. (Hmm, maybe they were giving him ideas?)

My kids weren't worried about socialization or dissecting frogs or algebra or even tomorrow's spelling test. They enjoyed hanging out with Mom, reading books, playing with scales (weighing scales, not snake scales), and hearing about huge whales that sing to each other in the deep blue oceans.

The more I hung out with my kids, the more I started thinking that way too.

You see, when I first started homeschooling, I thought it should be just like regular school...only at home. Cory was my guinea pig. I ordered a structured, highly advanced curriculum our first year, and I made him work through it—every lesson, every word. Math took an hour. Reading took two. I bought an old school desk that I made him sit at. Just practicing the spelling list took forty-five minutes—as did recess (for my sanity). We were both miserable.

It was impossible to be so structured once I started home-schooling Leslie and Nathan too. Teaching three children on three levels didn't work. The kids were cranky. I was crankier.

They wanted more time to run around. I felt as if I was running in circles.

So I prayed, *Lord, help!* He didn't change our day. He didn't change the kids; they were still as active as ever. He didn't transform them into baby Einsteins overnight. Instead, He changed me. And it all started with a spider.

I was sitting at the table, working on handwriting sheets with Cory and Leslie, and I could see the kids were getting restless. Cory's eyes were focused on the window, and I was sure he was daydreaming.

"Cory, finish up your worksheet, and then we'll work on your spelling words."

"Whoa!" Cory ignored me and jumped from his seat. He hurried to the side window by the door.

"Cory, you're not finished—"

The sight of the large, orange spider weaving a web in the window halted my words. Quietly, I followed Cory.

"Leslie, Nathan, come look," I whispered.

The spider, which had to be as big as a nickel, had just started weaving its web. With the grace of a ballerina, it swung from one corner of the long, tall window to the other. We watched as it worked with perfect precision. The morning sunlight glistened off the web, making it appear like spun crystal.

I'm not a fan of spiders, but I've never seen anything more beautiful. I forgot about the handwriting and spelling words and the other things on my list. Instead, I just watched.

"That's amazing." Cory's voice held awe. "How does it do that?"

"I don't know. Let's find out." For the rest of the morning we looked up spiders on the Internet. We drew pictures of our spider friend. We even went to the library and checked out books about spiders. And as we rode home singing "Itsy Bitsy Spider" at the top of our lungs, I felt this inner voice telling me, *This is what it's all about.*

Not that I didn't need lesson plans to teach math and science and writing, but that I could view our learning as a time of bonding and fun. It wasn't just about inserting facts into my kids' brains. It was about connecting with their hearts. The spider, which we called Charlotte, was just the breakthrough I needed.

One winter, I brought a beautiful hornets' nest into the house, only to discover in the spring that it was still in use. (The buzzing from its place on the kitchen counter was our first hint!) Crayon rubbings and framed prints still hang on my office wall—art-class projects that turned out half decent. My kids still complain about the video I made them watch on a shark dissection. And they still chat about their favorites of the books we read together.

Yes, my kids have learned, and I have too. Not only about the web-spinning techniques of spiders or the migration routes of monarch butterflies (both of which I learned as "the teacher"), but also how to interact as a family, to work through conflict, to share chores, to compromise, to have fun, to love learning.

Homeschooling my kids taught me that learning is a lifestyle, not an isolated event that culminates in graduation. It's a way of looking around me and thinking, *I wonder if…*or *what would happen if I…?*

In the choice to homeschool, I chose a challenge that still makes me ask myself, *What was I thinking?* at least once a week. There are days I'd rather climb into bed with a coffee and a good book than figure out another lesson plan. There are even days I'd rather scrub the toilets or clean out my fridge. It's then I'm forced to my knees. *Okay, God, can you show up today in a big way? I need you. We need you.*

And He does show up because, I think, God likes being needed. I needed Him a lot, to give me wisdom and patience and guidance as I trained tender hearts and filled young minds. I needed Him to guide my days and our school schedule. I needed Him to form me into the type of person who would be a good role model for my kids, who were watching me and learning from me 24/7. The only way I could teach them at home and survive day by day was to allow God to form in me some of that love, joy, and peace that comes from His Spirit.

While I don't believe homeschooling is for everyone, I believe that God led me to this choice in order to make me more aware of my moment-by-moment need for Him. Isaiah 46:9–10 says:

> Remember your history,
>> your long and rich history.

I am God, the only God you've had or ever will have—
    incomparable, irreplaceable—
From the very beginning
    telling you what the ending will be,
All along letting you in
    on what is going to happen,
Assuring you, "I'm in this for the long haul,
    I'll do exactly what I set out to do." (MSG)

I love this passage. Not only does it prove that history is important (yes, I used that with the kids too), but it reminds me as a mom that God is in it—all of it, every part of our lives—for the long haul.

After more than a decade of being homeschooled, my kids are fun to hang out with, and we enjoy each other. They are kind, thoughtful, and smart…most of the time. Not that homeschooling is a magic formula. After all, my house is never in perfect order, my kids still pick an occasional fight with each other, and they forget to feed the dog. They've had moments when they hated homeschool, hated me, and just wanted to be with their friends…but those days were few compared to the ones when we liked being together.

My decision to homeschool was a conscious choice to give my children time. Time to learn, time to share, time to grow up together. Little did I know how much the time would teach me. Little did I know how much God would draw my heart to His in the process.

K-MOM Frequency

It seemed like every busy mother's dream. My husband was going to a work conference in Florida for a week, and he invited me to join him. I had one day to play at Epcot with John and four days in a hotel room, alone, to rest, relax, and work on this book. Work, that is, when I wasn't lounging at the pool and sipping from my iced latte…*with* whipped cream. (It was vacation, you know.)

Five days with no dinners to cook, no piles of clothes to put away, no kids to shuttle around town. Yet it only took one day to realize that the things I was looking forward to getting away from are the things that have made me who I am.

Motherhood has stretched me…and I'm not just talking about the marks that my polka-dot bathing suit fails to hide. (With each child's birth my hips and thighs expanded along with my heart!) Although my physical body has changed since I've had children, my mental, emotional, and spiritual shape has been transformed even more. I think like a mom, have a mom's heart…and my ears are now tuned to K-MOM frequency.

While everyone seems to have a built-in warning system (part of God's standard package), only moms can recognize the little signal that goes off in their heads—the silent warning that tells them something's *really* not right and they *do* need to check on the lack of noise in the other room or the thump coming down the stairs. When I was home with toddlers, I was aware of every little noise, even when I didn't realize I was aware. I remember waking in the night, darting up the stairs before I was fully awake. I knew something was wrong. I knew I needed to get there, but I wasn't sure why.

Sometimes I found one of my kiddos having a bad dream. Other times it was a potty accident. Other times (my least favorite) I stumbled upon one of my kids throwing up. Once I even raced upstairs to find Leslie's friend—who had been staying the night—throwing up. Lucky me! It wasn't until after the mess was cleaned up, the child was taken care of, and the situation calmed that I questioned how I heard such a small sound so far away.

Even now, on vacation, I couldn't find the "off" switch. As I strolled through the theme park, I looked like a calm woman simply enjoying the park with her hand in her husband's and without a care. But, in fact, my eyes were fixed on the little boy who was trailing too far from the rest of his group. And the baby whose hat had slipped off her head, letting too much sun on her face. My ears were tuned in to the little girl's cries, seventy-five people back from me in line at the roller coaster. And I realized I could recognize a scolding in three different languages just by the tone of the parent's voice and the downcast look in the child's eyes.

Sometimes this radar can be a lifesaver—literally.

———

"Where are Dalton and Leslie?" I asked, glancing around. I don't know why I asked. John and I had invited our friends Charles and Katherine over for dinner, and their two kids were playing with our three kids. Katherine and I were chattering away when the thought seemed to come out of nowhere.

"Oh," Katherine responded, "I think I saw them head outside with the guys."

Our husbands, I knew, were capable of watching two four-year-olds…if they were aware that the watching had been turned over to them. I could have trusted that the guys knew the kids were outside, but something inside told me to check. And that thought was followed by another inner urging that told me to HURRY.

We found the guys talking and laughing. I scanned our yard and didn't see any sign of the children.

"Where are Dalton and Leslie?" I asked, not caring at the moment that I'd rudely interrupted them.

"We thought they were with you," John said. Then his eyes widened. "The river."

We didn't stand around to contemplate if the kids even knew to head that direction; instead we started to run.

"The river" meant the Flathead River behind our home. It

was wide enough for two boats to race down side by side. And deep enough…well, I didn't even want to think about how deep it really was. Especially now that it was at flood stage—high and fast. Even at night, the constant roar of moving water could be heard, filtering in through our bedroom window.

John ran down the trail to the river, and I followed. By the time I arrived, he was leading two children, one in each hand, lecturing the whole way.

My heart pounded at the sight of two half-naked children with wet feet who had been just seconds away from "going for a swim." It was so close. One minute longer, even thirty seconds more, and the story could have ended tragically.

My hands shook as I scooped my daughter into my arms. My lower lip trembled as I held her close. I could tell from the startled expression that she was upset because of her dad's scolding, but mostly frustrated that he'd interrupted her fun. She had no idea of the wild beating of my heart.

As John waited, I kissed her once, held her tight for a few seconds, and then sent her to her room for the rest of the night. Hoping our loving discipline would be enough to dissuade her next time. Praying my ear would always be so quick to listen to God's nudging and my heart so eager to respond.

———

Even though I've always had radar that warned me when something was wrong, I've not always listened to it. But motherhood does have a way of magnifying and intensifying our radar. Maybe because it wouldn't be just me who would have to deal with the consequences. If I messed up, made the wrong choice, did the wrong thing, my kids would pay.

So instead of ignoring the small voice that told me to check the seat belt one more time or take my son to the doctor (even though he'd just told me the previous day it was nothing to worry about), I did what seemed silly for the sake of protecting what was most precious. As the years passed I realized my mother's adage was true, "It's better to be safe than sorry," and so I checked and rechecked for no reason, especially when it came to the safety of my kids.

Some people claim that this inner voice or unsettled feeling is just the conscience at work. Cartoons display it as a little angel on your shoulder, pointing you the right way. I think of it as the Holy Spirit. God at work in me. It's a gift given to all believers. And unlike the crystal candlesticks I received at my wedding and haven't used since, it's a gift I've put to good use.

Yet for many years, I didn't understand this Spirit. I wondered why Jesus told His disciples—His best friends who had walked with Him, served with Him, and given up all for Him—that it would be better for them that He go away (see John 16:7). Then I realized that what Jesus was telling them was that He wasn't really going away. While He wouldn't be with them physically, His Spirit would be in their hearts always. This would be even better than His physical presence because storms or crowds or soldiers or distance could no longer separate them. The indwelling Jesus would always be with them, guiding them. It comforts me that Jesus is in heaven and in me—with me— speaking to me at all times, even as I live as a mom. Or especially since I live as a mom.

I've discovered that this God-given radar has morphed as my children have grown. I've learned to listen to the intricacies, tuning into the minor things that hint that something's not exactly right, such as when I see sadness in Leslie's expression. Or when Cory looks away a little too quickly. Or when Nathan seems fine, but that nudging inside tells me to ask…just in case.

In moments like these I feel God's Spirit telling me to stop. To turn off the computer, stop the housecleaning, or call my friend back later instead of answering the phone. Then the stop is usually followed by an urging to find a way to connect within this small window of time.

This happened the other day. Leslie had just gotten off work at a fast-food restaurant, and I was finishing up a long day of working at the computer. My eyes burned, my head was foggy, and I wanted fifteen minutes of quiet before I started making dinner. She entered my office and began jabbering about everything and anything. I listened for a few minutes, and then told her I was going to go lie down. She seemed okay with that and turned on her computer to check her e-mail.

I hadn't been lying down one minute when I felt that little stirring inside my chest. With a wisdom not from myself, I knew

Leslie needed to talk but just hadn't gotten around to the main point yet, so I rose, rubbed my eyes, and found her just where I'd left her.

"Hey, Leslie, do you want to drive into town and get some coffee?"

"Sure, really? That sounds like fun." Then she looked up at me. "But I thought you were going to go lie down?"

I shrugged. "Well, a venti latte will do the same job as a short nap. Come on, you can tell me about your day."

It wasn't until the drive home—after we talked about hamburgers and youth group and her need for new shorts and flip-flops—that Leslie told me about a struggle that one of her friends was going through and her own worries about how to deal with it. My daughter didn't need me to solve all her problems. She just needed me to acknowledge her struggle and promise to pray. The Spirit helped me show her that I do want to listen, that I do care.

These days I'm not so worried about my kids jumping into a roaring river or climbing too high or running away and getting lost. I worry about what's going on inside them: it's the things of the heart that concern me the most.

So I listen to that inner voice, which is God's Spirit. I turn my head when I feel a spiritual tap on my shoulder. I realize that these urgings are for my own good, not for my harm. For the good of the ones I love most. God's nudges point me to the best way, the best path—for me and my kids.

Chapter 7

The Squeeze
That Set Me Free

From the age of three, my daughter loved to ask questions. Why is the sky blue? How does a car drive? Where does the food go after you swallow it?

My answers were always short and sweet. 'Cause God made it that way. The engine makes it go. In your stomach.

My husband's answers weren't so simple. For example, the words he used in his explanation of where food went included *esophagus, digestive system,* and *waste.* And as John explained, our daughter listened intently, as if the explanation was the most interesting thing in the world. Then, from that moment on, she pointed out her esophagus to everyone she met, including the checker at the grocery store.

As my kids grew older, they continued to ask questions, but the questions became ones I didn't necessarily want to answer. When they were babies and toddlers, all they knew about me was that I was Mom. That was enough.

But then they started looking around and seeing that things didn't add up. They knew that life was made up of a girl meeting a guy, falling in love, getting married, and becoming Mommy and Daddy... "So, Mommy, why was Cory in your wedding photo? Are you really only twenty-five? Alina's mom says she's twenty-nine, but she's really thirty-seven." My kids got too smart too fast, and I had some explaining to do.

The truth is I just wanted to be Mom without having to reveal anything about my history. If I could have rewritten my story, I would have, partly because I carried lots of baggage, and I was getting tired of its weight. But mostly because I didn't want my kids to know about my past.

So when they got old enough to start asking questions, I wanted to tell them anything but the truth. A mom is someone who is supposed to set a good example, right? I wanted to be the mom they adored forever. I didn't want them to associate any bad thoughts with me.

The questions didn't come all at once. But they did come.

"Mom, where was I born?" Cory gazed up at me with large brown eyes. Leslie and Nathan paused from their play to listen.

"In a town called Mount Shasta."

"Were Leslie and Nathan born there too?"

"No, I had them in Redding. We moved there after Daddy and I got married."

"You had me before you married Daddy? I have a different dad, but you weren't married, right?"

Cory's question seemed simple enough, but how could I explain without going into too many details? Without telling him things that would hurt him more than help him?

"Yes, I got pregnant when I was in high school. You were a special gift. Then God gave me John to be your daddy and Leslie and Nathan's daddy too."

Heat rose to my cheeks, and I felt my stomach churn.

"What did I like to do as a baby?" Cory asked.

"You liked to climb." I tapped his nose with my finger.

"What about me?" Leslie looked up at me with a smile.

"You liked to be cuddled. I'd dress you up like a little doll and rock you."

"And me!" Nathan asked.

"You liked to wander away. I'd have to keep my eye on you, because you'd head off exploring and never come back."

Over time, I came to understand that my kids weren't judging me when they asked questions about their births and how they came to be. They just wanted to know. I didn't have to sit them down and spill my guts all at once. Instead, I was able to reveal things slowly, over time.

When Cory was six and John was preparing to adopt him, we sat Cory down and explained the difference between a biological father and an adoptive father.

I told him the basics about my pregnancy and his birth. I told him about my high school days and how I didn't have Jesus in my heart. I explained to Cory how he was a gift to bring me to God and also to John. He listened as I talked, and I could tell he understood.

John also explained how he'd chosen Cory just as much as he'd chosen me. And how he loved Cory.

"Yeah, duh," Cory said, giving John a hug.

So far so good. I hadn't had to tell my kids how upset and scared I was as I rode home from the doctor's office with their grandmother. Or that within a few months I dropped out of regular high school to attend a school for troubled teens, or that my life became a juicy piece of gossip to share at the doughnut shop or in the school hallways. These weren't happily-ever-after bedtime stories.

Even though I left that lifestyle far behind when I got married, moved to a different town, and started attending church, I still carried around the memories. They were like crumbs in my play dough. A few stuck to the surface but many more were mixed in and hard to see. Yet even though those crumbs were my secret, they were there. I still felt like that scared, embarrassed teen girl and could not imagine revealing my biggest secret to anyone.

A light fog hung outside the living room window, and the tree limbs outside appeared to be a delicate ice sculpture. The frosty, shimmering limbs fanned out like glass fingers, reaching. Although it was not yet 6:30 a.m., I'd read my Bible, jotted prayers in my journal, and spent time thinking about the year ahead. It was almost January. *A new year. New goals. My mom's birthday. And…*

"Sanctity of Life Sunday," I whispered the last four words and they lodged in my throat. I couldn't forget what Pastor Daniel had said to me, "Talk to me when you're ready to share your story…" I knew without a doubt this was something I needed to do…in the future. So I made a deal with God.

Next year, I'll share my story of healing that came from the post-abortion Bible study. Next year, I'll offer hope to others experiencing the same pain.

Then the tension in my gut tightened as I realized January was "next year."

No one else knows. I don't have to do it.

My promise was one I'd made with God but hadn't shared with anyone else, not even John. Yet the thought of taking it back pained me even more than the thought of standing in front of the church. Even though I hadn't heard the command with an audible voice, I knew this was something God asked me to do. I knew *not* doing it would be disobeying God.

I tried to ignore the insistence in my soul. *Are you sure, God? But then everyone will know.* John and I had finally found a church home—a group of people to serve God alongside—and now He was asking me to share my darkest secret. It didn't make sense.

Sunday came, and I tried to avoid all contact with Pastor Daniel. I succeeded in steering clear of him before the service, but afterward, as I strode down the hall searching for Cory, my luck ended. As soon as I saw Pastor Daniel walking toward me, I knew God had given me this moment. I knew what God wanted me to do.

When I told Pastor Daniel that I felt God was telling me to share my story on Sanctity of Life Sunday, he said, "I think that's a good idea. I've wondered when you'd be ready to share. I've been praying for you too. Why don't you write up an outline of what you want to say and e-mail it to me? I'll add some closing thoughts and share a few scriptures. Is twenty minutes enough time?"

Twenty minutes? It sounded like a lifetime. Standing up front. All eyes on me. Yet, I also felt a strength from beyond myself. "Yes, that will be good. I'll have my notes to you by the end of the week."

My life was being torn open. I knew God wanted me to share my story, but I would have preferred hiding my past mistakes. I wished I could hold His hand. I needed something to cling to.

———

I hated the idea of telling anyone my secret, and now I'd have to tell my kids about what I'd done.

I didn't want them to know I started dating when I was thirteen or that I faced my first pregnancy at fifteen. I didn't want them to know I'd had an abortion, continued to have sex with my on-again-off-again boyfriend, and then found myself pregnant again at seventeen. I especially didn't want Cory to know his biological father had wanted me to get an abortion or that he dumped me before Cory was born.

I worried that if my kids knew all the horrible stuff I'd done, they'd think they could do the same. Even more, I worried that they'd look at me differently. I'd be devalued in their eyes. They wouldn't respect me.

God was squeezing me, molding me into a woman willing to put her life and her kids into His hands. But I wished it wasn't so painful.

The day I was supposed to give my testimony in church, I sat my kids down and told them the things in my past that I'd been keeping secret from all but my closest friends. I told them how my darkened heart had thought about myself first over the first baby I carried. At ages ten, seven, and five they didn't understand what abortion was all about, but they understood they had a sibling who wasn't around and that Mommy was very sorry about that fact.

That's when I began to realize that I didn't have to have the perfect words or the perfect timing to explain everything to my kids. Even to Cory my past was just another story. Sure, it was partly his story, but the fact that he had two parents who loved him meant more to him than something that happened before he could remember.

Over time, I told my kids more stories. Sometimes because one of them asked, and other times because I thought they needed to know. Instead of them using my mistakes as an excuse for their own sins, the opposite happened. They witnessed my pain, regret, and struggle, and because of that, they developed high standards for themselves. They made positive decisions for their lives, in part because I was truthful about negative ones I made. And the things I wanted to hide forever are the things that showed them that I'm human, that God is big, and that there is nothing we could ever do to separate ourselves from His love.

It's hard not to pretend we are better than we are. We all want to look good—to ourselves and to others. We want to hide our imperfections. I wanted to hide my mistakes and sins—hide them all. But in the end what my kids needed from me was the truth. The truth of who I was and who I became because of Christ. They needed the truth of how wrong we can all go when left to our own devices. And where God can take us when we depend completely on Him.

The religious leaders in Jesus's day spent their lives modeling piety before God. The only problem was Jesus ratted them out. He pointed out the stuff they were hiding. He didn't let them parade around, making others feel bad, when these fakers had so many problems of their own.

But the religious leaders weren't the only ones who needed help. Even Jesus's disciples—the ones Jesus especially chose to walk with Him—messed up a time or two. They fought with each other. They longed to be God's number one man. They didn't believe when they should have. They ran away when they needed to stand.

Yet they were the ones who experienced the risen Lord first. They were the first spokesmen of the Savior.

Sometimes those of us for whom God has done so much do the best at telling the truth about Him. Yet God isn't content with a partial transformation. He sees the stuff we want to hide and knows how much more beautiful we will be if we deal with the crud.

After I told my story on Sanctity of Life Sunday, a crowd of people surrounded me. Hugged me. Thanked me. Told me their stories. Cried. There were more stories within our congregation than I could have imagined, and I thought I was the only one. My story had given them hope for *their* stories.

My goal during my kids' fundamental years was to become someone my kids could look up to, emulate. I thought this would happen if I could serve God by influencing the world through writing. But maybe God had something else in mind. I realized that He did want me to be an influence, but perhaps not in the way I thought. I felt both humbled and excited.

I also realized there were more things I still needed to deal with. Emotions I'd tried to hide. Pain I'd attempted to ignore. Answering questions reminded me that my life—and my heart—were still works in progress. Telling the truth about my past forced me to revisit those dark places. And as I did, I prayed about those memories, and I turned them over to God. I cried over the pain. I cried for the young woman who was looking for love and found heartache. I saw myself in God's eyes—saw the ways He'd tried to draw me to Him. I saw what darkness had done, and I understood my choices as the natural result of sin.

For many years I'd believed God had forgiven me, but as I studied His Word, I realized I needed to forgive myself. It was hard, but I did it. And as I felt the freedom that came with forgiveness, I shared with others—in church, in Bible studies, in my community. I discovered that kids need a mom who trusts them enough to open her heart, to confess her mistakes, and to ask their forgiveness for the loss of their brother or sister who's missing from the family tree…at least in this lifetime. To show them that messing up isn't the end. It's the beginning. It's where God's grace is needed. And where God's unconditional love is found.

Yes, my play dough may still get crumbs, but it's not my job to hide them or even to pick them out. God is faithful in doing that. It's my job to be truthful about the dirt that still lingers and to hand myself over, plopping my blue, pliable self into His hands.

Chapter 8

Brightening the Blue

I believed a break from the routine—working at my computer, shuttling kids, cleaning the house—would be a boost. I
thought a day of fun would give me some extra oomph. Instead,
I felt heavy and lazy. And it wasn't only because I'd eaten too
much—red-bean ice cream from China, crème brûlée from
France, and soft drinks from Israel, Spain, and Japan.

If my soul was a color, that day it was blue. On some days
blue represents bright, cloud-free skies. On other days, somber-
ness and sadness. Blue is beautiful in van Gogh's painting *Starry
Night,* but there are days in real life when it doesn't have the
same quaint, classy feel. Far from it.

I had an unsettled feeling deep in my chest—the same feeling I had when I said a rude comment about my neighbor's
overly active kids, only to discover that my words had gotten
back to her. It was a sense of uneasiness, mixed with regret,
mixed with disappointment in myself, warning me that something wasn't right.

Lord, what's up? Why do I feel so heavy hearted? I paused as my whispered prayers caught in my throat. Deep down, I knew what was wrong. Because I was on vacation, I'd been lazy about my spiritual health, excusing myself because I had been working so hard and needed to get away and simply relax. I had made time for ME. I'd even found time to write *about* God, but I hadn't made time for God. I hadn't been putting Him first. God wants my faithfulness…and I need Him. Even red-bean ice cream can't take the place of the quiet moments when I read God's Word, sit quietly, and wait for Him to speak to my heart. Fun rides, character sightings, and interesting exhibits cannot replace the settled, joyful feeling I have when I take time to meditate on God's goodness and write down my thoughts of Him in my journal.

So I opened my Bible, having forgotten where I'd previously left off, and started reading in Matthew. I read about Jesus and considered how God came to earth. *God.* I let my mind wander, thinking about the marvel of that. In my contemplation, I also realized that God wants to live and work *daily* through us—His followers—but we, the very ones who claim to love Him, often don't invite Him into our lives. How much more active would God be in this world if His children made time to put first things first? How much more active would He be if *I* did that?

Because I've been close to God over the last dozen years, I feel the ache of separation. But I haven't always been so spiritu-ally sensitive. During the years when I was just getting to know

God, I often went weeks ignoring His invitation to spend time with Him.

———

It was at the end of a busy month. Cory was just one year old, and I was taking classes at our local community college. A white-capped Mount Shasta loomed overhead on a beautiful fall afternoon, and I watched my son as he played in the front yard of our small apartment complex. I flipped through a schoolbook, but my mind was replaying the soap opera I'd watched earlier that day. Would Bo and Hope end up together? It's a question I'd pondered for the past five years and one yet to be answered.

Then the thought hit me: *It's been weeks, maybe months, since I've made any time for God.*

Cory turned and tossed the small rubber ball to me, but this time instead of catching it, I let it drop to my feet. I was stunned. I'd been sending my husband off to work every day with a kiss, dropping my dear child off at day care so I could attend college classes for a few hours, cleaned, studied, watched TV, hung out... When was the last time I'd spent some time alone with God or even prayed? I couldn't remember.

It scared me. How could this be? My mind went back to a few years prior. I'd been a misguided teenager, heading down the wrong path without a care for anything or anyone except my own pleasure. I thought I'd changed—that God had changed me. But if my life had truly been transformed, how could I forget the One who had forgiven and restored me? It was far too easy to forget, drift away, and revert back to living for myself.

I'm still afraid of getting forgetful. Of doing my own thing and going my way too often. Of putting God on the back burner. But I'm a lot better about tuning in to these feelings of distance. My struggles these days have more to do with paying attention to the warning signals that something in my spirit needs attention. I don't know why I haven't figured this out by now. It's not like the signs are hard to decipher.

The uneasiness starts like the first rumble of an empty stomach, although it's not my stomach that's rumbling. It's my heart. My mind is distracted. My thoughts unfocused. I know I need something, something different from what I already have. My feet shift. My knee fidgets. And I think I need a nap. Or maybe a snack. Or maybe a new pair of shoes. Discontentment builds, and the crank on my crankiness gets wound tighter and tighter. A tense feeling builds in my chest, and suddenly all I can focus on is the fact that my kids are making too much commotion.

Just a few weeks ago, I chewed out my daughter for checking her e-mail before starting her homework, even though I let her do that every day. When I saw Leslie's reaction and realized

I was turning a little issue into a big deal, I took a step back. I escaped into my bedroom, shut the door, and sank onto the floor on my knees. And then I thought and I prayed and I tried to dig up what the real issue was.

My feelings of discomfort aren't always due to a lack of time with God, prayer, or Bible reading. Sometimes, they're a warning that I'm trying to please everyone and handle everything in my own strength. It's me running out of fuel and expecting to run on fumes, when instead I need to be filling up with God.

Some days I just need to make time to do that. To pull over and fill up. To ask God to seep into every part of me. But there are other times when I try to do that and it doesn't seem to work. And then, no matter how many praise songs I hum or Scripture verses I read or devotional thoughts I replay in my mind, I can't get filled up by God. The things I'm ignoring form a tangle of debris that clog up the access ducts to my heart. It's like the clog in my vacuum cleaner after I tried to clean up all the needles from the Christmas pine. Even though the machine looked great on the outside, the clog blocked the flow.

The sun crested over the mountains outside my living room window, yet the rays seemed cold. I took a sip of my morning coffee, but even that brought no joy. I put my coffee down next to my Bible on the side table and sank to my knees. The house was quiet as my family slept, and I could hear the beating of my heart within my ears.

God…show me. What gives?

He immediately brought to my mind an interaction I had with a man from our church earlier that week while at the grocery store. The man had laughed at my jokes and admired how I looked. He even bragged about my books to another shopper. A smile spread across my face and my chest warmed. I could have excused myself, but I was enjoying this handsome man's attention. It made me feel special. I'd even thought about him again later that evening, wondering where else I might be able to "run into" him.

And then I remembered that I'd purchased some new clothes online, clothes I didn't need but bought because I was feeling down about my weight. If I had some fun new clothes, I'd look better and feel better, right? So instead of turning to God to fill me up, I'd gone shopping.

It wasn't that I'd intentionally set out to fill myself up with things. It just happened as I was going along my merry way. No, nix that. These things don't just happen. They keep on happening.

Maybe they go back to my feelings of wanting to be appreciated, adored. Maybe somewhere inside I still feel like that awkward, pudgy junior higher or maybe that little girl who longed for the love of a father. Maybe I haven't completely dismissed the emotions of the teenage me who was pregnant and ashamed.

Maybe my "fixes" stem back to those habits of trying to make myself look better than I felt inside. It isn't until days later, when I feel a void deep within, that I realize something is amiss.

The biggest problem with these "minor" things is that they're things God talks to me about time and time again. They are issues I refuse to think are serious, just like the time I didn't think the clunking noises in my car's wheels were that serious. (Five hundred dollars for new brakes and drums should have changed my notion that little problems don't cost much to fix.)

When I ignore my feelings of uneasiness, I get cranky and impatient. I can put on a good show with my colleagues and friends. I can even do an okay job of hiding my frustrations from John. But I spend most of my time with my kids. And since I'm the big person whom they are supposed to respect, listen to, and not talk back to, I often get away with much more with them. After all, what are they supposed to do—put Mom in the corner until her attitude improves?

I grew up in a household where I often had to weigh my parents' attitudes before I opened my mouth. Over the years— after being in the middle of breakdowns and flareups—I became a pro at judging who was happy, who was mad, and what I could get away with in light of those facts. I don't want my kids to have to always weigh my attitude. I don't want to ride the waves of my emotions that explode outwardly when I don't take care of the unrest inwardly. I've seen what can happen.

Whenever I hear myself being short or crabby or irrational, a single image comes to mind. It's the memory of my interaction with four-year-old Cory. He'd been sitting at the dining room table practicing writing his name. The rest of the day is a blur, but I do remember reaching for his hair, to brush it back from his face. He reeled back, wincing. I was offering a loving stroke to my son, but that hadn't always been the case. Like my parents before me, I'd gotten into the habit of flicking Cory's shoulder or slapping his arm anytime I was frustrated. And the littlest things—like his walking too fast, talking too loudly, or eating too slowly would set me off.

"Stop that."

"Be quiet."

"Don't!"

Just remembering Cory's reaction fills my eyes with tears. I don't like confessing that that's how things were for many years. It would be easier to ignore this ugly side of me, to hide it.

But Cory's wince woke me up to a problem. It forced me to consider how I was treating my son and how he viewed me. It made me realize that if my attitude or my words or my actions weren't right, then I needed to take a step back, get away, and deal with them, instead of letting my negative emotions bubble their way to the surface and onto my children.

I don't want my kids growing up with the same insecurities

and hang-ups I had. I want them to understand that it is possible to be mad or frustrated or overwhelmed and still control one's feelings and actions. An angry flick on the arm isn't okay, especially when my child is on the receiving end of my angst.

It doesn't matter how I was raised. It doesn't even matter that my own parents' mixed-up reactions make it hard for me to deal with my own. Those things are in the past—I can't change them. What I can change is my own actions and reactions.

While it's easy to recognize when we are letting our emotions have free rein, it's harder to control them. I'm so glad that Jesus never asked me to handle everything—my habits, my reactions, and my weaknesses—on my own. Instead, Jesus tells me to depend on Him. One of my favorite verses is John 15:4: "Live in me. Make your home in me just as I do in you. In the same way that a branch can't bear grapes by itself but only by being joined to the vine, you can't bear fruit unless you are joined with me" (MSG).

Only when I depend on my connection with Jesus can I do the things He asks. Only with Jesus can my life produce fruit, good things to bless and feed those around me. When I connect with Jesus, He comes in and fills me and deals with all those heart problems that are beyond my ability to fix.

Jesus knows the blue feelings I have when I've spent too many days away from Him. These aren't feelings of guilt but rather emptiness that comes from missing God's presence. He reminds me to make time for us to get together, not only because He takes pleasure in meeting with me (which He does), but also because He knows He can do a work where I am weak.

I'm not perfect as a mom, and I never will be. Instead, I'm learning to heed the warning signals. I'm learning to not turn up the radio and ignore what's going on inside me. It helps to remember that my kids are riding with me through life, and I want to make it an enjoyable ride.

When my heart is turned toward God, when I abide in Him and give Him space to work…peace reigns. Blue brightens. And the warning signals fade.

Chapter 9

Carrot Oop

I can barely make out my daughter's laughter from across the coffeehouse. Her friend is moving to Florida, and Leslie had asked for a ride to meet her for coffee. Another friend met them, and as I glance over at the three teens, I notice they're absorbed in the moment—the coffee, the cream cheese Danishes, and mostly each other.

It's not my nature to take time for such moments, for girl time, fun time. But I'm getting better. I'm trying to schedule an afternoon every week with a friend for coffee or sitting at the lake or strolling around the mall. At least a few nights a week I play a board game with my kids or we watch a movie together. On weekends I create space for a short hike or bike ride around the neighborhood.

I have to remind myself to take time for fun, especially when there is so much I want to do. I tend to think God works through…well, work. I have to remind myself that sometimes He speaks most clearly when my mind isn't filled with the list of all I need to accomplish in the next five minutes. God didn't create us for work alone. The fact that He gave us laughter is proof of that. Sometimes we just need to take ourselves less seriously and simply relax and enjoy our life, our kids.

The scent of freshly baked bread drifted into the living room from the bread machine in the kitchen, yet even the yummy, yeasty scent didn't give me peace. I should have been practicing addition facts, reading to my kids, or working on crafts with them, but I wasn't in the mood. That day I'd received another rejection letter. Would I ever see my writing dream fulfilled?

Just that morning, I'd whispered a prayer, asking God to make me *want to* turn over all the areas of my life that I was still clinging to. As I prayed, I turned over my clenched fists, lifting my hands up in the air with open palms, not because I felt I could completely give up my dream, but because I wanted to, was trying to.

Brightly colored cloth draped the couch, the dining room chairs, and bar stools. The kids slipped in and out through the fort door, checking to make sure they had everything just right. I listened to their whispered conversations, wondering how they could find such pure joy in simple things. I envied that.

Nathan's blond head peeked out, and he looked at me. I waved from my spot on the couch. He smiled and darted back inside. His muffled giggle sounded from underneath the blankets, and I knew if I could bottle and label childhood joy it would be worth millions—no, make that billions—of dollars.

I laughed out loud and pushed the pile of schoolbooks to the side, knowing I wouldn't get to them that day. Suddenly, making sure Cory read the right number of pages and filled in the correct worksheets didn't matter quite as much. My sour mood lightened.

I had a beautiful home and three great kids. I had an amazing husband who believed in me and supported me, despite all my hang-ups. I had a good church. A good life. And as I sat there, watching the children play, I remembered that God loved me like I loved these kids—even more. He didn't need me to accomplish great things. He loved me just because I was His. I also realized that it was He who would be doing the accomplishing, not me, in His perfect time.

I curled to my side, content with watching the kids play, remembering that many of my dreams had been fulfilled. The knowledge of God's pleasure drifted down on me like dandelion puffs floating on the wind. As certain as anything around me—the velvety feel of the couch cushion, the laughter of my kids, the warmth of the heat coming from the stove—I felt God's smile, as soft and light and cozy as the warmth in the room.

"Mama, you wanna come in our house?" Leslie asked.

"Okay." I wiped my tears and climbed under the blankets. It was more spacious in there than I thought.

"Here is your bed." Cory pointed to a pillow. I curled up in a little ball, tucking the pillow under my head.

As I lay there, enjoying the feeling of little hands tucking their blankets around me, I considered that the perfect examples of willing hands and feet were Jesus's disciples. Where did the Savior of the world find His helpers? Not in the temple among the priests. Not in the colleges of Jerusalem. He found them on the seashore mending their nets. Or at the tax collector's booth. And sometimes they found Him from the invitation of a brother or a friend.

And it wasn't all about work with Jesus. He took time to rest and get away from the crowds. To have dinner with friends. Surely the Son of God could have spent every day, all day working. But He, too, enjoyed the laughter of little children as He told the disciples to let them come to Him.

"You have a pretty good house here." I patted Cory's shoulder. "Where did you learn to build such a nice house? Who taught you that?"

"You did. 'Cause you're my teacher," Cory stated matter-of-factly.

"But I never taught you this. I never taught you how to move the chairs around and drape the blankets so they don't fall."

"But you taught me other stuff. And because I know other stuff I know this, too."

I thought about Cory's statement, and in a strange way it

made sense. God had been teaching me about the balm of a child's laughter on an aching soul and that His pleasure can be felt, but not necessarily understood. Because of those lessons I was learning how to do this mom thing better too.

"You hun-ger-ey?" Nathan asked.

"Yes, are you going to make lunch?"

"I'll make lunch," Leslie said with all seriousness. She brushed her hair from her face and climbed out from under the blankets.

I heard her in the kitchen, opening the cupboard, opening the fridge, turning on the faucet. She was quite confident for being only four. As I listened, I immediately knew what she was making. It was a special "lunch" she made for Nathan at least once a week.

I listened to the scraping of the butter knife on the plastic cutting board as she cut the baby carrots into chunks and plopped them into hot tap water.

Nathan peeked out to watch. "Carrot oop." He nodded in approval.

"Oh boy, carrot soup." I rubbed my belly.

Cory and Nathan worked to add another "room" to the house-fort as Leslie finished "cooking." And as I lay there, I wondered why I didn't do this more often. Just enjoy my kids and play with them. It was easy for me to think about doing things for God, but the idea of just *being* and enjoying the simple joys of life was hard. My mind struggled to stretch and wrap around the concept of play and rest as two of the good things that God had designed for me on earth.

I also wondered why I didn't seek God more or trust His voice. It was almost as if I assumed He would pick hard things for me to do just to make me suffer. It was difficult for me to realize His plans for me are good, just as baths are good and healthy food is good and schoolwork is good for my kids. Yet God's good is even better. He not only knows what's best for me, He loves me completely.

What amazed me most was understanding that God knew about *today*. He saw me there, lying under those blankets, laughing with my kids, thanking Him for His goodness, sensing His smile. He KNEW. He knew rejection and failure would be hard for me. He knew those things would stir up old insecurities. God also knew that I would be changed because of them.

I thought again of Jesus's disciples. There were moments their impulses led them to great faith—like Peter's leap onto the waves at Jesus's command. But their purity came as they walked with Jesus. As they feared for their lives and wondered why Jesus said what He said and did what He did. Their hearts were changed when Jesus pointed out when their motives weren't right and when their actions were outright wrong. They were different men than they started out being, mostly because they went through tough stuff. Yet their thinking also changed, and they became different men when they understood that Jesus's plan was different from their own. And when they learned that moments of joy were possible even during the tough stuff…when they witnessed the glory after heartache and Jesus's presence after loss.

Why hadn't I realized sooner that my life wasn't just about me? It never was. It never would be. Life wouldn't always turn out as I wished. And I guessed there would be more moments that I'd feel as if all my dreams were dashed to the ground. But it was then, I was discovering, that togetherness was most precious. It was then that God's presence was carried perfectly on the laughter of a child.

"Carrot soup is done," Leslie called in her singsong voice. I stood around the table with my kids. We couldn't sit because our chairs were occupied, holding up our pretend home.

There were four bowls, four spoons, four napkins, and four smiling faces. I ate my soup. It was only carrots and hot water, but I didn't care. These were my kids and this was my life, and carrot soup had just made it to the top ten of my favorite foods.

Chapter 10

Trust and... No Way

No two kids disobey in quite the same way. Cory, my oldest, was very sly and could get away with a lot, but he couldn't handle the guilt. He's the one who'd wake me up at 6:00 a.m. by standing by my bed and staring at me. I would know as soon as I opened my eyes that he'd done something I'd told him not to.

"What did you do?" I'd ask.

The answers varied: Got into the cookies. Wrote on the wall. Stole his sister's candy.

Half-asleep, I'd tell Cory his punishment, such as no television for the day, and then he'd let me drift back to la-lá land. How easy. Unfortunately the other two children had styles of their own.

Leslie's style was that any request would yield an immediate no. She'd make excuses for why she didn't need to do what we told her to do. She was dramatic. She'd cry and pout. And after two hours of arguing and tears and being sent to her room to think, Leslie would realize that she did want to obey, and she'd do as asked. Sigh.

Nathan, on the other hand, has always been very agreeable.

"Nathan, clean your room."

"Yes, Mom."

"And after that feed the dogs."

"Yes, Mom."

"And then take a bath and get dressed."

"Yes, Mom."

The problem would come when two hours later the room was still a mess, the dogs were still hungry, and the kid was still wearing his Thomas the Tank Engine pajamas. And when I confronted him, the excuses followed. "I was just going to do that," or "I forgot" were two favorites.

My kids remind me of the sons in Jesus's parable in Matthew 21:28–31:

There was a man who had two sons. He went to the first and said, "Son, go and work today in the vineyard."

"I will not," he answered, but later he changed his mind and went.

Then the father went to the other son and said the same thing. He answered, "I will, sir," but he did not go.

Which of the two did what his father wanted?

"The first," they answered.

Jesus understands human nature. He knows the way we handle instructions is really a heart issue. Moms understand this on a daily basis. The instructions we give our children aren't just about the tasks we want them to complete or the guidelines we need them to follow. They're also about our kids learning to listen, respect authority, cohabitate with others, and obey when they're told.

I deal with the same things my kids deal with. There are days I realize I've messed up, and I immediately turn to God. Other days I have good intentions but don't always follow through. Some days I whine and complain. Eventually, after many tears, I give in to what I know God wants from me. These whining sessions don't happen often, but most of the time they involve key moments when I know God is asking something from me, and it is the last thing I want to give.

—

"Tricia," my friend Kathy called to me as I walked through the Wednesday night supper line at church. "Are you still able to make it to the meeting tonight?"

I shook my head. "I've thought about it, and I just don't have time to add another thing to my schedule."

I started to move on, but Kathy persisted. "Well, could you come and give us some ideas? You're a great idea person." She gave me a smile that said "please."

I relented. Surely I had time to brainstorm a few ideas. What could it hurt?

Five of us tucked ourselves around a folding table and discussed the venture at hand—the start of a pregnancy care center in our area. The ideas came easily enough. Whoever started the center would begin by offering free pregnancy tests and counseling, then they could expand to include baby items for mothers in need.

Still, the project seemed huge. Overwhelmingly so. Where would the financing come from? Would we have enough volunteers and leaders?

When it came time for our Wednesday night classes to begin, I stood up to leave.

Pastor Daniel stood too. "Can I talk to you for a second?"

"Sure."

We stepped to the side.

"I'm wondering if you'd be interested in helping to start the center? You know, to get it going?" He didn't mention my own experiences with teen pregnancy. He didn't have to. I knew what he was thinking.

Still, my plate was officially full.

But looking into Pastor Daniel's face, I couldn't tell him no. Instead, I gave him the "churchy" answer. "I'll pray about it," I said. "Then I'll get back to you."

The next morning, as promised, I prayed about the venture. My prayers centered mostly on a way out. I prayed for an easy way to say no. *God, you know I'm busy raising kids and writing. I'm helping people all over, God. Help me find a way to get out of this.*

I sat and listened, and amazingly I felt a stirring in my heart. *What are you doing about the people in your own community? How are you helping them?* It wasn't an audible voice. It was a quiet thought that I knew wasn't from me.

I sat still for a minute, unsure I'd heard right. Help start a crisis pregnancy center? Was God really asking me to do that? That would be a huge undertaking. It would put my writing on the back burner. Just when I was getting used to my shape, God stretched me. Squeezed me.

That's how I knew it was God.

I thought about my passions. Starting a nonprofit organization was not one of them. Yet, as I prayed more, instead of feeling a release from this ministry, God brought to my mind even more reasons I should become a part of it. He reminded me of the lies I heard when I went for counseling during my first pregnancy. The heartache of abortion. My past experiences as a teen mom.

These young girls and women need someone who understands. Someone who's been there.

Throughout the day, the more I waited on God, the more He showed me that He could use my past pain for *His good.* He reminded me that my help and effort could keep some teens from having to face the despair that plagued me for so many years. I could give hope to others, hope I did not receive.

I tried to absorb what God was asking me to do. I went through the day crying, pouting, and trying to talk myself out of it. It didn't work. I called Pastor Daniel to tell him I would help with the pregnancy center, and as I did reality sank in. Launching a new ministry would take time away from pursuing my own goals. My own dreams...all my hard work...would come to nothing. And what about my kids? Cory was ten. Leslie was seven. And Nathan, my baby, was five. How would this decision affect them? Wouldn't launching this center take time from their schooling? Take time from them?

God, are you sure?

When I finally got tired of fighting God, I told Him I'd follow. It was more a reluctant surrender than an excited acceptance.

Yet just because I dragged my feet didn't mean God dragged His. Within a matter of months, we had fifty volunteers, a donated building, and a large sponsor base. In the first year we were open, abortion in our town decreased by one-third. More than that, God showed me what He could do when I was willing to place my life and my circumstances in His hands. I found joy in helping others. As I talked to young girls about making good choices, as I handed out diapers and encouraged worried and overwhelmed women, I discovered the statement is true— it's better to give than receive. And this working knowledge changed my shape. My heart *did* start to look more like His.

And what I didn't realize was that God wasn't only shaping me...He was at work shaping dozens of other people with the same desire to help the cause of life. He also was shaping the community to notice and support women in need. I just happened to be one of the people He used to start His work.

And to think I could have missed it all. I could have stuck to *my* plan for my life and missed God's heart.

When it came to obeying God, there was, of course, one big decision: *I will help launch a crisis pregnancy center.* But it was the small steps of obedience that made all the difference. The small steps included making phone calls, meeting with women, and designing brochures.

For four years, the center was my focus as I wrote grants, trained volunteers, and started young-mom support groups. I even taught teens the importance of being abstinent before marriage. What seemed like a fork in the road at the time turned into a major highway of ministry for myself, my family, and my community. There are no side trips on God's path.

Today, I have an advisory position at the center, and the ministry continues to grow. And although God led me to join Him in the launch, He showed me that when we take care of His business, He takes care of ours. As the ministry grew, my kids participated in the serving and caring. As God molded me, my interaction with our community molded our kids. Their vision expanded as they saw the needs of others. They discovered they could help people in small ways and that little things done in love could make a big difference, not only for the people they could help, but in their own lives too.

I've been able to see more of the lessons my kids learned as they have gotten older. In fact, now they're the ones coming to me with examples of God at work. Just last night Leslie talked to me about the advice she was able to give to a friend who has been sexually active but who is also wanting to make a recommitment to purity. Leslie told me how she talked with this girl and prayed with her. My mother's heart was warm and happy—not only because Leslie's friend had someone to talk to, but because Leslie is walking in the direction I'd been leading her, the walk of obedience.

Chapter 11

Martha Doesn't Live Here Anymore

I stepped over dog throw-up as I was going down the stairs the other day. My mind was deep in my work assignment, and I was running downstairs for a cup of coffee. I didn't want to lose my train of thought, so I called to Nathan to clean up the mess for me. (*His chores do center around the dogs,* I justified.)

Eight years ago if someone had told me I would do that, I would have accused them of defamatory statements. If they had shown me a photo of what my desk looks like today, I would have insisted it was someone else's desk, not mine. I was the woman who picked fuzzies off the carpet as I walked through the living room. I had every photo in an album, and I started making my own Christmas cards in September.

I used to be a closet perfectionist. You could come to my house anytime during the week and find the closets clean. And the floors. And the toilets. During those days, the color of Ty-

D-Bol as it swirled in beautiful blue around the rim was my idea of entertainment. I shared the joy of my shining bowl with my friend Mr. Clean. He always smiled at that. As a matter of fact, he always smiled.

But being a closet perfectionist wasn't just about my closets.

Do you know those e-mail questionnaires that come around every so often? What's your favorite color? (Green) What was your favorite TV show when you were ten? (A three-way tie between *The Brady Bunch, Gilligan's Island,* and *The Flintstones.*) What was the last thing you ate or drank? (Coffee, coffee, coffee.) If you could be anything, what would you be? (This was easy. I wanted to be perfect.)

I wanted nothing more than that—to be the perfect wife, the perfect mom, the perfect housekeeper, the perfect hostess, the perfect writer, the perfect child of God who would make Pollyanna look like a Hell's Angels biker. I wanted to make everyone happy, 100 percent of the time.

I parked in the single-car garage, unbuckled the kids, and grabbed the groceries. I'd told John to invite his new co-workers for dinner that night. Even as I did, I questioned my own motives. Had I invited them so that everyone at work, new guys included, would know what a great wife and mom and cook and housecleaner *I* was? And how lucky John was?

Three voices trailed me, and the smile that played on my lips straightened.

"Take off your shoes. Hang up your coats."

It was the same drill we'd had since moving into our house. The "no shoes in the house" rule started, in fact, the day we signed the mortgage.

I kept my three kids occupied with a brand-new Veggie Tales video. I'd been saving the DVD for an occasion such as this. Every mother knows a *new* movie ensures rapt attention for three straight-through plays. I also knew that was far too much television consumption for three young minds ages two to seven. I knew this because of my "perfect mom" voice, which was quick to point out my every fault.

I looked at the clock, and my heart started to pound. There was too much to do and not enough time. I tried to appease my worried mind by telling myself the guys *would* run late. I told myself there *would* be time to bake a cake and cook the chicken and set the table and do everything else that needed to be done.

I read through the chocolate cake recipe again, wondering why I'd decided to make a cake from scratch. Panic was in full force. It was the recipe my friend Kelly made for us when she invited us to her house. She told me it was easy, but I'd forgotten that she was the one who also made to-die-for cheesecake, also from scratch.

A person who wasn't attempting to portray a younger version

of Martha Stewart would have picked up some cookie-dough ice cream as a backup. But as I whipped up the batter, I *knew* that even if I had cookie-dough ice cream in the fridge, I would make the cake anyway. I had an impression to make. I didn't always cook like this, but I liked people to think I did. That was one of my issues. Or maybe every other issue revolved around this one. The only problem was that even when I got it all right, it still never seemed like I'd succeeded.

The minutes ticked by, and everything took longer than it should have. I moaned as I pulled the chicken out of the fridge and discovered it was still frozen. Desperate, I threw it into the microwave to defrost.

When I heard car tires crunching over the gravel in the driveway, I was far from done. The cake had been baking for twenty minutes and the chicken was thawed and ready to be dipped in the breadcrumbs, which meant dinner wasn't near ready to be served.

And then, to add to the panic, when the front door opened I realized something was terribly wrong.

The pungent odor of burning chocolate hit my nose just as I heard the footsteps in the foyer. I opened the oven door to see that batter had poured out over the sides and had burned to a hard, black blot-spot on the bottom of the oven. A smoke cloud puffed from the open door as if Puff the magic dragon was hiding inside. I flipped on the hood fan, but I wasn't fast enough. Within seconds the smoke alarm blared.

The guests slipped off their shoes, with curious looks on their faces, as I opened the kitchen window and wildly waved two potholders in the air, trying to clear the smoke.

Calling to the front door, I joked about trying a new recipe. I smiled as I flapped my arms, but I knew John could read the angst in my eyes. All I could think about was the stories that would circulate around the office the next day. The laughter. The unflattering first impression I'd made.

An hour later, chicken was served. Forty-five minutes after that, I served the second cake I'd whipped up. The food tasted good, but it had the same effect on my tight jaw as if I'd been chewing cardboard. *Next time I'll get it right.*

Later that night, I lay in bed at John's side with feelings of unworthiness settling on my chest. It was heavy, and felt like the whole Rocky Mountain range.

I really, really wanted to be the one whom everyone looked at and thought, *Isn't she amazing? How does she do it?* But God wasn't concerned about that or about how content or organized I was. He wanted to do some closet cleaning of His own, a spring cleaning like I never expected.

When I was at home, taking care of my little world, straightening shoes and dusting the top shelf of my kids' closet (which wasn't really dusty due to the row of perfectly arranged stuffed animals), I convinced myself that my life was completely in order. I had so much daily stuff to think about, I didn't realize I hadn't dealt with some of the pain of my past. I'd simply swept it under an end table, added a doily and vase of flowers on top, and pretended it wasn't there.

But the day God called me to help open the pregnancy center, all that began to change.

As I worked with young women, my past helped me to connect with them because I related. Seeing the struggles of the teen moms reminded me of my own, and I began to relive the pain. When a young woman lamented about never knowing her father, pain shot through my heart. I ached with her. When I saw boyfriends dumping girlfriends and girlfriends two-timing boyfriends, all the drama of my teenage years came flooding back.

God had seen what I couldn't—chunks of toughened emotions that were the result of hard circumstances. Nuggets of pain that had solidified and ruined my pliancy. He knew I couldn't be formed into the right shape until He took out the hard spots in my heart.

I wanted to help these girls, but for many of their struggles, I had no hope to offer. I couldn't truthfully say, "One day you'll stop thinking about your dad," or "One day you'll no longer feel the shame of teen pregnancy," or "One day you won't have any memories, or longings, or questions about your old boyfriend." For me none of those things had happened. And I honestly didn't know if any ever would.

In order to give these young moms hope for peace and healing, I had to find it myself. This, for me, meant writing out my emotions, my prayers, my pain and taking it all to God. When I wrote things like, "I'm twenty-seven years old, and I'm still struggling with emotions I have for an old boyfriend," I wondered if my kids would read them someday and what they would think. Yet I knew it was better to get my feelings on the page than to carry them around.

As I turned those things over to God, He spoke to me about them through His Word, reminding me of His love, His forgiveness, and His desire to wash me white as snow. As I held each of my hurts before Him and said, "Here you go. I'm done carrying this around," He picked out what didn't belong and poured living water on the bits of hard dough.

As I prayed and surrendered, I felt God's pleasure. I felt His smile upon me when I shared with teen moms that I still had the same issues but that God was cleaning my heart. The more I gave...to others and to God...the cleaner I felt.

It's been said that a messy house is evidence of a messy heart, but it was just the opposite for me. The more I got my heart in order, the more God urged me to move beyond my safe, happy little world. After I started volunteering, my perfect house didn't remain so perfect. Instead of scrubbing the tub until it shined, I trained volunteers and helped to remodel our new center. My kids couldn't keep up their rooms because they were working beside me, folding blankets and stacking diapers.

As the weeks and months passed, something else started happening. The more I served God and saw Him working in lives, the less concerned I was about a dust-free existence or with how others saw me. I didn't need to impress anyone else because deep down I felt God's approval.

Now I'm comfortable if the floor only gets swept once a week or the mail stacks up for two. My clean heart equals a messy house, and you know what? I'm okay with that. I used to hide the truth—my struggles, my feelings of insecurity—in the back of my perfectly arranged closets. But not anymore. Now John tells me I don't have any skeletons in my closet—because I display them on the lawn.

While I don't like seeing dog puke and stepping over it or watching the tower of laundry topple over as I head out the door, I've come to realize that those things don't matter as much as people—whether it be the people in my house or those in my community and my world. Like my friend Twyla says, "You fight dirt your whole life and then they bury you in it." The fight to have everything clean will always be a fight, but it's a fight that we can tackle with the wisdom of God. Wisdom to know when enough is enough.

Someday, in eternity with God, things will be perfect. But until then, the only areas that will even come close are those spaces that we open up and allow God to fill.

Chapter 12

His Word Is There
When I Knead It

I 'm the worst math teacher ever. Just ask my kids. Even though I advanced as far as trig in high school, I'm clueless about how to explain mathematics to my teens. I justify this by saying that, although my kids think square root is an exotic type of carrot, they can tell you that Uriah the Hittite was one of David's mighty men and that Ishbi-Benob was a giant who would have killed David had it not been for Abishai's rescue. (If Ishbi-Benob had succeeded, everyone would know that name!)

That they now know these biblical facts isn't a credit to me. Although I grew up in church (my mom attended, my stepdad didn't), I'd never studied or even read the Bible. But when I had kids, God began to speak to me, deep in my gut, insisting I take time to plant truth (and some really good/crazy/interesting/ unusual Bible stories) in the hearts of my children.

I wanted to be like Jesus, but still I struggled with finding time to spend with God. Then one day I realized I often complained about not having time to read my Bible and pray, yet I made the time to do other things I wanted to do. So the next day when my alarm went off, I decided to read my Bible first. *Five minutes should be enough time,* I figured.

Even though my motivation was to ease my conscience, God began to speak to me from His Word. Five minutes turned into fifteen, and soon I started understanding what the Bible was all about. My little date with the Good Book became a romance with my Maker.

I got myself a journal and jotted down all the Scripture verses that stood out to me. Sometimes I added my thoughts or other important things I learned. Other times written prayers.

As the weeks passed, I added some devotional books to my morning time and then Bible studies, such as Henry Blackaby's *Experiencing God.* Wow! I found some good stuff. Before I knew it, I grew to need my time with God. Just me and Him and a cup of java. God spoke. I listened.

Each moment we spend in God's Word, we're kneading truth into our lives that we can pull out and use later. The truth is like those little brown sprinkles of yeast that need to be woven into bread dough. (Yes, I've made bread at least twice; I know these things.)

We can add God's Word to our day, but it does not spread and expand unless we put it to use. When something happens that makes me angry, I remember, "In your anger do not sin," and so I hold in what I want to act out. This is the kneading.

The kneading also happens when I want to read the book that I know I shouldn't be reading. I think, "I will set before my eyes no vile thing," and I throw the book in the trash instead. Experiences like these work the truth into our hearts as we work them out through our circumstances.

The cool thing is that once those truths are worked in, they find their own place to nestle into our hearts. They're there to stay. It's like the survival pack I used to stock in my car. Inside a simple tote bag in my trunk, I kept snacks, juice boxes, kids' stories on tape, books to read, and extra clothes (for those potty accidents that always happen in the middle of the grocery store). And after a while, I came to depend on these supplies. Kids hungry? No problem; have a granola bar. Boring ride to town? Pop in a book on tape. Got muddy on the playground? Lookie, extra sets of clothes.

As we work truths in and live them out, they become our survival packs for the next moment we may need them.

I wanted to tuck God's Word into my children's hearts so that they could access it when they needed it, but it was much harder than I thought. Just feeding my kids, dressing them, and making sure they put only edible things in their mouths was work enough. Yet providing them with truth they can turn to during different times in their lives is far more important than dumping some goldfish crackers into a plastic bag. One lasts for a moment. The other for a lifetime.

Just last week I noticed a piece of paper taped to our family's bulletin board. It was in my daughter's handwriting: "Have I not commanded you? Be strong and courageous. Do not be terrified; do not be discouraged, for the LORD your God will be with you wherever you go" (Joshua 1:9). When I saw her pinned-up scripture, I thought of two things.

First was the compromise we've come to with Leslie. Lights out *can* be extended if she's studying God's Word. She's growing into a young woman who's in love with God, and I want to do all I can to support her in this. The second was an image of my kids at ages three, five, and seven, lined up on the sofa, reciting Psalm 100. It was a typical fall morning, and they were excited to recite a whole chapter of the Bible together. It didn't matter that they couldn't read the words or that they had no idea what "we are his people, the sheep of his pasture" meant. They were proud of their accomplishment. I was too.

Through the years, Scripture memorization has been a part of our family life. Although I wish there were secrets to make it easier, I have none. It just takes doing it. Sitting down with the Bible and getting the kids to repeat my words, over and over and over. Sometimes I wrote the verses out on cards, other times I didn't. Sometimes we'd all be in a good mood and have smiles on our faces as we said the words. Other times we did it when we were tired and cranky and would rather just veg in front of the TV. But either way, the important thing is that the words stuck.

After Psalm 100, my kids memorized Genesis 1. (This came up as we studied the origins of life in science.) And after that our Scripture memory followed the flow of our lives. I knew that if my kids were dealing with issues such as anger, pride, and lying at ages four, six, and nine, they'd be dealing with the same things at fourteen, sixteen, and nineteen. (And I was right, they are.) Like those little sponges that grow in water, life issues enlarge in severity and importance as a child's world expands.

Not that I did things perfectly. Sometimes I'd get so busy that I'd let weeks (or months) go by without spending time with my kids and the Bible. There were times I didn't take advantage of their enthusiasm. There were moments when I was so concerned about big issues that I missed small opportunities to help my kids apply God's Word to their lives. But looking back I can see a habit, one with many starts, stops, and stumbles, but a habit all the same.

I had the kids memorize Luke 6:27–28, "But I tell you who hear me: Love your enemies, do good to those who hate you, bless those who curse you, pray for those who mistreat you," because the words made it hard for my kids to be mad at their brother or sister when I forced them to recite the words during any altercation. (Seriously, it worked!) I had no clue that these very verses would be kneaded into my own heart as well.

My heart trial began after I posted a chapter from one of my books on an online forum for teen moms. They were eager to read it because it was for them. All went well for a few hours, and then one false rumor lit their online world on fire. The frenzy started when one of the young moms accused me of using quotes from their forum without permission. Some of the quotes in my book were similar to ones that appeared on the forum…that's because I corresponded with a few of the young moms and they answered questions for me. Yet one young mom was certain that if her friends were quoted in the first chapter, then I must have stolen quotes from all of them—including her—and used the quotes throughout the book.

My heart was crushed. The very girls I'd hoped to help were saying horrible things about me. Hate mail filled my inbox. After reading page after page of their angry comments, I put a movie in for the kids and locked myself in my room for a good cry. In the midst of my tears, a Scripture verse floated to the front of my consciousness: "Love your enemies, do good to those who hate you, bless those who curse you, pray for those who mistreat you."

Do good to them? Bless them? Pray for them? I knew this was God's message to my hurting heart.

So I did. I prayed for these young moms—young women who were hurting and angry at the world, just as I'd once been. As I did, my hurt transformed into compassion. I continued praying, blessing, and doing good as best I could, and through it all I discovered a love for these young women that stood through the fire of their criticism. It wasn't the shaping I'd wanted or expected, but it was one I felt thankful for.

Years earlier, as I followed that nudge from God to hide His Word in my kids' hearts, I knew it was a good thing, but it was only after this experience that I realized that the same words had been hidden in mine as well. More than that, I realized that while knowing God's Word is necessary, the power of the Word of God comes out when the words are applied. Life lessons come about when God's Word is lived out. I'm learning that, and my kids are too. Through this hiding, we're thankful for the truth we can turn to, truth that is kneaded deep inside our hearts.

Chapter 13

In Noodles and Novels

M y daughter, Leslie, wore new jeans, a black T-shirt, and a star necklace on her first day of public education, which was today. She turned sixteen a few months ago and is taking classes this semester at Flathead Valley Community College. The Running Start program, which allowed her to get both high school and college credits for the same classes, was too good a deal for her to pass up. As soon as I mentioned it to Leslie, she was gung-ho. She had no worries. It was an adventure!

Our family has had a lot of adventures lately.

Last week one of the first things Cory told me about his recent missions trip to Mexico was that he had preached at a church with a translator.

"Yeah, Mom, when we were talking about our week, I knew that if they asked me to preach, I was supposed to do it."

"And they asked?"

"Yep." Cory shrugged. "So I did. I spoke on Paul's message to the Ephesians, and it was amazing."

It was Cory's first time preaching and his first time speaking with a translator. Two firsts in one day.

I've taught my kids that they can do anything they set their minds to. I didn't do it with lots of pep talks or self-esteem stickers. In fact, at the time I didn't realize I was teaching anything at all.

———

"A verb is a word that shows action or a state of being." I read the grammar rule from Cory's worksheet page to him. His eyes glazed over, and he glanced longingly at Nathan and Leslie, who were playing with toys three feet away. I hate to admit it, but my eyes glazed over too.

We'd been reading and memorizing and "doing school" for more than two hours, and I wondered how long was long enough. What did other kids do at school all day? Should Cory be reading chapter books by now? Should Leslie be counting to twenty? Was I just being paranoid? (Uh, yes!)

Deeper issues plagued me even more than addition and phonics woes did. Things I was afraid to share with anyone else for fear of being labeled a bad mom. I loved my kids. I enjoyed time with them, but sometimes I wondered if this was all there was to life.

Was this all my days were going to be for the next fifteen years? Raising kids, cleaning house, cooking easy meals, and considering a trip to the grocery store an exciting outing? And, of course, asking myself deep questions like, *How many times a week is it okay to eat mac 'n' cheese before it causes nutritional deficiencies?*

I told myself that all of this—caring for these kids—is what will matter in the future, while at the same time I deflated my own desires and dreams, tucking them into my pocket like a limp balloon.

I considered another spelling rule I'd taught Cory a few days before, "Use *i* before *e* except after *c* or when sounding like *a* as in *neighbor* or *weigh*." But as a mom *I* rarely came before anything. *I* was taken care of "after."

After the baby is weaned.

After the kid is potty trained.

After he can read well.

After she is grown and gone…I will _____ (fill in the blank). Read more, volunteer, give, care, grow.

Of course, the "I will…" also dabbled in more immediate things. After a strong cup of coffee. After mealtime and playtime and cleanup time and reading time and (dare I hope?) nap time. Then I would consider following my dreams. It would be foolish to try to do so any sooner, right?

I read to Cory a little bit longer, but the feelings of anxiety wouldn't go away. Not anxiousness, as in worry. But anxiousness as in I wanted to put a little time into the work project that kept circling in my mind like an airplane looking for a place to land.

Yet the notion of sitting down for even ten minutes seemed impossible.

I ignored the image in my mind of "the good mom" who bakes cookies with her children and creates things like papier mâché globes and elephants and flowers with them every day.

The inner urges wouldn't ease up, so I decided to give myself thirty minutes to get my thoughts on paper. But first I prepared the kids.

I got out the coloring books and crayons and set them on the small table in my office. I put kid songs in the CD player. And the kids were excited.

Yet ten minutes later, they were swarming around me again.

"I'm hungry."

"I'm thirsty."

"I'm bored."

At first, I gave in. Apple juice and vanilla wafers around. But during the second round of pleas, I put my foot down.

"No, I'm sorry. You're just going to have to wait. It's mommy time, so try to play or color or…something…for thirty minutes. Please?"

My hope was that these little snippets of time would add up to a big chunk of something that resembled my dreams. My hope was that I could balance being a mom with following my passions. Would trying to do both be worth it? Or would it all just be a waste of time?

The mail had become the highlight of my day. I'd just sent off a lot of magazine articles, and I was eager for good news. Cory, at eight, was old enough to ride his bike around the loop to the mailbox.

My days went something like this:

10:50 a.m. "Cory, honey, can you go get the mail for me?"

He smiled, and I could tell my request made him feel big, old, useful. He plopped down by the front door and slipped on his Power Rangers sneakers, firmly fastening the Velcro, before hopping onto his bike.

10:52 a.m. I stared at the lawn and beyond, seeking the first sign of Cory's return.

10:57 a.m. I paced up and down the driveway, worried that my anticipation for an acceptance letter had put my son in danger, although I didn't know what type of danger it could be. The worst thing was I couldn't see him from our house.

I thought back to me at Cory's age, walking my brother home from kindergarten. I'd leave my class, walk to his, and wait until he was dismissed. Then we would head home. And it was a long walk—at least two miles—and included crossing a set of train tracks and strolling down Main Street, where anyone could have pulled over and snapped us up. If Ronnie and I survived that walk, surely a trip to the mailbox would be okay.

Cory's okay. The mail's just late. He's just waiting for the carrier to finish sorting everything into the right boxes.

11:00 a.m. I spotted the adorable boy on his little red bike. The wind blew dark brown hair back from his face. His cheeks were red from exertion. He parked near the garage and slipped off his backpack, holding it out to me as if it were pirate booty. A twinkle lit his eyes.

"Well done! You are such a huge help. Wow, you really can ride fast on that bike."

"Yeah, I could prob-lee beat Dad in a race."

"You just might. Maybe you should try tonight after dinner," I suggested.

I nonchalantly flipped through the items in the backpack. Bills, note from grandma *(oh)*, note from mom *(ah)*, postcard from dentist *(ugh)*—there it was, an SASE, a self-addressed-stamped envelope. They are used mostly because publishers don't want to have to spend their hard-earned money on postage in order to tell you that they don't want your stuff.

I slid it open. It was a rejection of an article. My heart fell. Maybe next time?

I'm sitting at my desk, and music by Third Day is playing in the background. My kids like to hang out in my office because that's where their computers are. They do research on the Web or watch movies or play games. Sometimes Cory is editing a video he's shot. Other times Leslie's editing photos she's taken. Nathan is often drawing his own cartoons or working on the novel he's started. And in the middle of everything else they're either texting or IMing or finding some way to connect with their 201 friends.

For years I thought I was giving my kids the raw end of the deal by creating mommy time every afternoon so that I could pursue my dream. What started as thirty minutes turned into two hours, and during this time Cory, Leslie, and Nathan had to learn to entertain themselves. Sometimes they'd play with each other—pretending they were doctors or that they worked in the grocery store. Sometimes they read. Sometimes they drew.

I got the first inkling that maybe I wasn't being the "bad mommy" I thought I was when I heard complaints from my friends.

"My kids don't know how to entertain themselves. I have to read to them or play with them all day long."

And soon after that I started getting praise from people around town, at the doctor's office or at church. "Your kids play well together. They seem to enjoy their siblings. How did you do it?"

Uh, I gave them no choice. They had to spend time together daily while I followed my dreams...

I wrote for many years before ever getting published. Those years I worked in faith, believing that God had a plan and that

He had stirred my heart for a reason. It was during that time I clung to the words of Hebrews 11:1: "Now faith is being sure of what we hope for and certain of what we do not see." I wrote with faith that maybe my words could make a difference. I wrote in faith that taking a little time for myself wouldn't ruin my kids forever. And I'm happy to say it hasn't.

There were times my kids needed me, and I put aside my work to be with them. But as the years passed, they came to understand that I was up to something when I clicked away on my computer. They *really* started understanding when they saw copies of magazine articles with my name on them. (And they got super excited the times when they saw their names in print too.)

And later when books with my name showed up on our doorstep, they started talking about the books they wanted to write, about the subjects they enjoyed. I realized then that they'd been paying attention even when I didn't think they were.

They'd been watching. Learning.

While my kids played in the same room, they'd obviously been keeping an eye on what I was doing. They saw me working away, using my time well. They also saw me tackling more than I thought I could. They saw me believing in myself and trusting that if God led me to a project, He would help me. And most important, they saw me pursuing my dreams, and they saw those dreams coming true. They saw that life could be an exciting adventure. And they saw that anything worth having was worth working hard for and persevering, even in the face of disappointment.

Now it's a joy to see my kids trusting that God gave them dreams so they could make a difference, and believing that hard work will pay off—whether it is taking college classes or going on missions trips. Like me, they are discovering that God is big enough to complete what we can't possibly achieve on our own.

My kids didn't raise themselves. Not even close. I've been there for them—as a teacher, as a bus driver, as a cook, and as a listener. And when I'm not running around with them, attending their games or heading out on a bike ride with them, they know where to find me.

You see, the kingdom of God is in my 12x12 office, where everyone congregates. Jesus finds pleasure *here*. He's also with me when I leave my office and venture into my day, whether it's in my noodles (made with love) or my novels (made with love).

To my kids I'm Mom, whether I'm cook Mom or writer Mom or teacher Mom or taxi Mom. And doing things other than parenting doesn't make me any less of a mom. It took me awhile to figure that out. It also took me awhile to figure out that God's help isn't limited to one area or another. He's faithful to pour His love through me. And I wouldn't have it any other way.

Chapter 14

The Church That Needed Us

Last week our pastor put John and me in charge of the evening church service, which focused on our recent missions trip to the Czech Republic. He had some crazy idea that it would be great if we placed two couches on the stage and talked with fellow team members about our trip as if we were chatting in our living room (media slide show included!). As I sat on the stage and looked out at the congregation, it was like looking into the faces of my family members. My husband, kids, and I are who we are because of these people. I truly felt at home on the stage, in this church.

From the moment God got hold of my life, I knew I wanted to raise my kids in the "right" church. Women from my grandma's church had shown me what love is all about, what a true body of believers looked like. Their care for me reminded me that God cared too. But finding the right church isn't always an easy thing.

Immediately after our move to Montana, we attended a

church I loved. It had lots of people, exciting worship, and preaching worthy of its own national radio broadcast. Yet no matter how often John and I tried to get involved, we were turned away. We volunteered for children's church, only to be told our help wasn't needed. We tried to connect with a small group, only to be told it was full.

We sought and didn't find.

Then one of John's co-workers invited us to his church. The first time I attended the church I now consider my church home, I cried. Hard. The congregation was too small. The worship too old-fashioned. The message too ordinary. It's not what I'd wanted at all. It wasn't what I was looking for. I wanted a church that had a lot of younger couples. This one didn't. I wanted a church with a great children's church service. This church had none. Yet I knew without a doubt it was the church we were being called to.

People approached us right away. They asked about our family and invited us to be a part of their lives. I felt like a missing piece that had found the right puzzle, yet something was wrong with the picture. Why had God connected us to someplace that didn't look as if it fit our (my) needs? Why had He placed us here? Didn't He care about my preferences?

———

We'd been attending our church for a month when I invited Pastor Daniel and his wife, Vickie, over for dinner. Since we were contemplating becoming members, it was only natural that Pastor Daniel wanted to get to know us and hear our story.

We talked for a few minutes about our move to Montana and about the ways God had answered our prayers, and then Pastor Daniel turned the conversation to a subject I had anticipated.

"Speaking of a church home…that's one of the things I wanted to ask you about. Do you know how you'd like to serve? Do you have any passion that God's put inside you?"

I balled my fists on my lap and then released them before the pastor noticed. Service to me was a double-edged sword. I loved donating time and doling out my effort, but I also knew the cost. In California, John had been so busy serving at church that I sometimes felt like a single mom for weeks and months at a time. John was an elder. He helped with the books, and he taught Sunday school. He helped to walk the church through a church split. There were many weeks when he was gone during the evenings because of church activities, and I didn't want to go there again.

I also was aware of my own tendencies to want to please others, sometimes to the detriment of my family. I volunteered in the nursery, and I attended a couple of Bible studies. I was hospitable to others, but I'd gripe for the three hours it took to clean and get ready. Sure, I was a perfect hostess, but sometimes at the cost of being a good mom.

Yet, I knew there *was* something on John's heart. Something he'd been talking about since before our move.

John's eyes brightened at Pastor Daniel's question. "Actually,

I noticed you don't have a children's ministry. It's been on my heart for a few years to start a dramatic children's church where we act out the Bible and then do additional application skits. We can have lights and music and really make the Bible come alive for kids!"

The pastor was quiet. It was one of the first times I'd seen him without words. Finally, a smile curled his lips. "John, Tricia, I've been praying about this very thing for three years. You have no idea how you're an answer to prayer. There is another couple I'd like you to meet—Kenny and Twyla. They've talked about something like this too, but didn't want to tackle it alone."

A chill ran down my neck and my arms, settling in a cool, bubbly pool in my gut.

John's jaw dropped. "Actually, we know Kenny and Twyla well. We've been taking a parenting class with them. They're great people. I had no idea Kenny wanted to do this. He never mentioned it."

"And you didn't mention it to him, but are you surprised?" Pastor Daniel looked as if he was ready to leap off the couch. I wanted to hide under it.

Just then I heard a crash upstairs, and I excused myself to check on the kids.

They were fine, and the crash—I discovered—was a tower of blocks that had "reached the sky." The tower was smashed, and now my kids were building an ark. I smiled, realizing their play involved re-creating some of the Bible stories John had recently read to them.

"Good thing you didn't get hurt when the tower fell over," I said. "It could have been dangerous."

Instead of heading right back down, I waited. I processed. For some reason I always needed to process. I glanced around the room.

My kids shared a large room with three beds tucked in three corners, reminding me of the sleeping arrangements for Snow White's dwarves. Shelves filled with books occupied the fourth corner of the room. Colorful posters with nursery rhymes hung on all the walls. Boy, girl, boy clothes—from large to small sizes—hung in the closet.

The previous year in California, I'd never imagined we'd live in someplace so nice. Before this, we'd always rented low-income apartments. Now we had a three bedroom, cedar-sided house next to a beautiful forest. And instead of worrying about how to survive and meet this month's bills, John had a great job as a computer tech, and we were enjoying a little breathing room. I was glad that Montana had given John space to dream. More than that, to make his dreams real.

He'd talked about his idea for a dynamic children's church for years, even when we didn't have a church home. I'd always listened, like I listened to all John's dreams. I even told him I'd help if the time ever came for something to happen. And now…

Why did my body suddenly feel weighed down by the thought of it? Why was my mind whirling like a toy spinner in the wind?

Maybe the thought of volunteering week after week overwhelmed me because it sounded like another thing to manage. More work. More kids. As if I didn't spend every moment with children.

Yet I couldn't help thinking about what I wanted most for my own kids: a church where they could become excited about God, where their faith would grow. I realized that as a mom I couldn't always pick what I'd enjoy the best. I realized that church wasn't designed to make me feel good, to be waited on, and to be taken care of. I needed to think of my kids' needs above my own desires. And I had a feeling their needs would be met if the ministry John was planning did take off.

Maybe church wasn't supposed to be a his/her ministry thing…but an "us" ministry thing. In the past, John and I had done our own things, heading our separate ways. But as I thought about working alongside him in children's church, suddenly it didn't seem so bad. We'd be giving our kids, and other kids, a way to learn about God in a fun way. And more than that, we'd be doing it together.

Sometimes the things you think will do you under are the very things that show you God is real. The very things that show your kids He's real too.

Last Sunday during a free moment, I sneaked to the back of our church's multipurpose room. One hundred children sat on a carpeted floor. In front of them, colored lights illuminated a stage. Carnival music played in the background as actors modeled the importance of being a Christian on the inside, not just acting like one on the outside. Although a dozen actors (I use that term loosely) including myself participated, my eyes focused on four—my husband and my three kids.

My kids grew up in what we named W.O.W. (Wee Ones Worship). We just celebrated our eleventh year. If that isn't a miracle in itself, I don't know what is. If I'd had my way, this ministry would never have begun. It was John's dream, not mine. Yet I'm so glad I supported him.

As soon as he started getting our kids involved (when they were just young kiddos themselves), they caught the vision. Every Sunday, we shared the good news of Jesus through drama, puppets, and song. We started with twenty kids, and then the church grew. Young families started attending. Unchurched people found Christ. They also found a place to call home. Our church became the type of place I'd been looking for. I just wish I'd known sooner that had been God's plan all along.

I have to admit there are times when I don't feel like going to church and acting. Maybe I had a busy week. Maybe I'd been running and running without a break. But the weird thing is that I've learned it's the times I don't feel like serving when service works best. When I'm at the end of myself, God steps in. He takes over. His love flows through me, and by the end of the presentation, I'm the one feeling excited and empowered.

It's hard to stay grumpy when I gaze out and see one hundred kids singing and dancing for God. It's hard to consider giving it up when week after week kids are able to express not only the previous week's Bible story, but the Bible stories for the last two months and the personal applications for each one. God loves little children, and it's hard not to feel that love as I serve them.

We videotape our program every week. I'm not sure why. Maybe to chronicle how funny we look getting dressed up in Bible costumes and chef hats and as first graders with spinning hats and lollipops (my favorite). Sometimes we pull out an old video just to watch. We laugh at how young everyone looked (including John and me). We revel in how much fun we've had over the years.

Sometimes you do what you have to do (even dressing up in funny costumes and volunteering every week) for the sake of your kids, even if it means more work. And sometimes you discover in the middle of it that God had something for you, too. I'm just glad that God is a God who *sees*.

God saw potential in our little family and called us to take on the task of making the Bible come alive for kids. God saw the dozens of little people, especially my own kids, who needed to hear God's Word.

God saw the church that needed us. God saw our hearts and how we needed this church. He showed us how blessed we are when we serve, and He knew how we'd be served in return.

I thought I knew what I wanted. Instead God knew what I needed.

I love that He does that.

Chapter 15

Stretch Me,
But Not My Kids

I n every person's life there are people who stand out. Like the
lone, flashing *open, open, open* sign on a dark and empty street.
My first, only, and favorite childhood Sunday school teacher was
that to me. Tall, red-headed, with a laugh that caused you to
smile, Margo lives in my memory.

Margo loved God, and she opened her heart to our small
class. I remember when she took me to a Christian bookstore
and gave me ten dollars to spend because I'd memorized verses.
Another time I won a dinner out with her at a Chinese restaurant, and she let me pick out anything I wanted on the menu. I
chose sweet and sour chicken and fried rice, and I felt quite special as I finished it all myself.

One year my gold stars earned me and a friend a night over
at Margo's house and a shopping trip. I felt important because
someone who wasn't my mom, wasn't a family member, wanted
to spend time with me.

Looking back, I wonder what she thought when she found out I was pregnant and that I'd dropped out of regular high school. Did she feel like a failure? Did she wonder if she could have done something more to help me?

I remember when I first started dating, she came to me and talked to me about "that boy." She knew I was heading down the wrong path, and she tried to warn me. And what did I do? I ignored her. I did what I wanted. I seemingly turned my back and walked away from everything she'd taught me.

Yet I didn't think of the pain I caused Margo until I started reaching out to help others, just as she had reached out to me. When I started helping people, I realized that there are those who don't want to be helped—those who will do exactly the opposite of what we advise.

But when I really understood, and when I really hurt, was when my kids were on the receiving end of the pain. I can handle people messing with me, but don't mess with my kids. And there came a point when I questioned if God really knew what He was doing. Should I really encourage my kids to give and serve if it meant they'd be trampled and crushed?

We had just started our Teen Mom Support Group meeting, and there was a knock at the door of the large Victorian house. I opened it, happy to be there serving.

A local church had given the house to Hope Pregnancy

Center for free. More than fifty volunteers had spent months remodeling it. My kids and John helped too. They'd joined me as we painted and cleaned and folded baby clothes. They watched with amazement as the center's every need was met. They rejoiced when money came in for carpet just when we needed it, when furniture was donated for our counseling room, when the bathroom was remodeled by a local church. And when a dozen women volunteered to mentor teen moms, my family encouraged me to be a part. Together, we praised God for His goodness, and soon my passion became theirs. It was clear to all of us that this was God's work. My kids became passionate about prayer, about seeing God work, about making a difference.

A second knock sounded, and I opened the door of the house. A young girl stood there. She was almost my height with dark, short-cropped hair. The laughter of the other teen girls drifted out from behind me.

"Are you here for the meeting?" I stepped aside and welcomed her in.

"Uh, I guess so. My dad dropped me off. He told me he'd be back in two hours."

"Are you pregnant?" I looked at her stomach and thought I saw a slight baby bump.

"Yeah," her eyes widened. "I just found out."

"Then you've come to the right place. This is a support group for teen moms. I'm Tricia."

"I'm Kassy."

We entered the living room. It was packed with young women who'd come for advice, encouragement, help.

Older women, caring volunteers, talked with younger women. Some of the younger ones had babies on their hips. Others still carried them inside. I gave Kassy a name tag.

"Every week you'll earn Mommy Money for attending, which you can use to buy diapers and clothes for your baby from our stocked store. We have a free dinner and child care here at the meetings too."

Kassy looked uncertain as she joined the others for dinner.

"Okay, we better get to the main event," I said as we finished eating.

I felt a tap on my shoulder and turned. Leslie stood there, holding a fussy baby on her hip. The baby's mom had just turned sixteen and was living with her boyfriend, who was the same age. The mom had been one of our first attendees and had invited all her friends to the pregnancy center. Leslie was eleven and one of our best baby-sitters.

"Mom," Leslie said. "I'm looking for the pacifier. Do you have it?"

I patted my front jean's pocket, remembering I'd held the baby earlier. I felt a lump and pulled out the pacifier. "Here you go. Sorry about that."

I gave Leslie a quick peck on the cheek. "Good job, girl. You are a natural with these kids."

Leslie grinned and strode out of the room. She felt important, because she was. I needed her. The moms needed her. And I could see from her face she felt God's pleasure.

—

The first time I took Leslie to the pregnancy center as a volunteer, I wondered if I'd made a mistake. I wanted my kids to learn to serve others, but was she ready? Would it be too much for her? Girls not much older than she was talked about who they'd slept with, what they'd done the week before, and what they planned to do. It was far from a tame environment.

Things went well at first. The teen girls were nice to Leslie, and they treated her like a little sister. Leslie and I had some great talks on the drive home. She and I talked about the girls, and we talked about their choices. I shared with her how each of us desires love and sometimes—especially when a girl comes from a harsh family background—she starts looking for love from guys.

"Yeah, but now look at what they're dealing with," Leslie commented. "They have to worry about taking care of their babies and making their parents happy. They go to school, and some of them work, too."

As I glanced over at Leslie's wide eyes, I knew I didn't need to lecture her on how purity—or choosing not to be pure—affects every part of our lives. She saw the truth of that lived out in the young women she met.

Some days I was sure Leslie wouldn't want to go and help, especially when her dad and brothers were planning fun events, like dinner out or a movie night. Yet even during these times, she came and served. Taking care of babies was hard, but feeling the appreciation of the young moms who were able to get two hours to interact with others like them brought Leslie great joy.

But as she got older, the young moms started seeing Leslie as someone who could make their lives easier.

"Leslie, my favorite little sis, would you be interested in baby-sitting tomorrow? It's only for an hour, and I'll pay you. I promise," LeeAnn, one of the girls, asked.

Leslie loved the kids, and she had a hard time saying no. "Okay, sure. I'll be home."

It made me happy that Leslie loved helping others, but I had a nagging worry, too. I'd been helping out teen moms for years, and I knew that sometimes things didn't turn out exactly as they promised. So when she told me about baby-sitting, I asked her, "Are you sure you want to baby-sit? I thought you were going to Jayme's house."

Leslie insisted she did, and that it would be for only an hour.

Sure enough, the next day the baby-sitting lasted longer than one hour. It stretched into two, three, and then four. LeeAnn had plenty of excuses, but no money for Leslie.

"I promise I'll pay you next time."

"Oh, okay," Leslie said in a weary voice.

"Well, that didn't turn out like we planned," I said watching the young woman drive away. I glanced at Leslie, and I could see the disappointment on her face. I knew she enjoyed helping, but she'd been hurt by the teen mom's flippant attitude. It hurt my heart to see someone taking advantage of my child.

I know that when I reach out to people, things won't always turn out the way I'd hope. There are some people who will take advantage of my kindness. There are others who will reject me. Even worse, there are those who will mock my efforts. And to tell you the truth, I'm okay with that. Jesus was rejected over and over. God says to "seek first his kingdom," and leave the rest up to Him. And when I face disappointment, I simply hope that next time will be better.

But when my kids are the ones who are hurting, I want to tuck a blanket of protection around them like I did when they were small. I want to protect Leslie's heart. I want to stand guard, watching to make sure she stays safe. Yet should I do that? Should I protect my kids like that?

I've learned that when I feel called to give and serve beyond my ability and even when I get nothing in return, I discover my need for God. If I can handle everything myself, then I don't need Him. Giving without thinking of oneself is a wonderful *and* scary place to be. Maybe it's a lesson my kids need to learn too.

It's been even scarier as my children have gotten older and God's call on their lives has taken them to faraway places. (Having a teen mom mistreat my daughter seemed like a minor thing compared to knowing they were traveling into a foreign country on a missions trip without me!) I know God can take care of my children better than I can; it's just my heart that struggles. There comes a point when knowledge of God's protection only goes so far.

Recently when Cory announced he felt called to serve God in Mexico, helping in street ministry, part of me panicked. Street ministry is dangerous. Mexico is far away. And Nathan, who's only fourteen, is already talking about serving as a missionary in Europe.

I felt stretched as I heard the news, but I also felt a stark comfort. It was as if God's Spirit inside was telling me, "This is what you trained them for. They want to care for people and share My good news. What could be better than that?"

Yes, I want my kids to learn to be God's servants—to be givers—but it's unnerving to think of them traveling to other countries and heading into unsafe situations without me. It hurts my heart to think of the rejection they'll face. The struggles. The heartache. The mom in me wants to keep my kids safe. To provide for them. To meet their needs. It's easy to give myself; it's harder to give my kids.

It's easy for me to see how discomfort and challenges transformed *me,* but I still wish my kids would have an easier path. Handing them over to God is easier said than done. Over the years I've become used to God throwing me into the unknown.

I'm used to the shaping and squishing. I'm okay with stepping out of my comfort zone. But the truth is, I don't want my kids to go through discomfort. When they were little babies, I swaddled them just so. I checked for lead-based paint and made sure their toys weren't choking hazards. I liberally applied sun block, and I enforced wearing hats and mittens to keep off the cold.

Yet I know that while giving and serving and reaching out to others isn't easy, it is where we meet God and experience Him in ways we can't know within our safety zones. That's what I've discovered.

So in the end, as I watch my kids follow my footsteps, I'll observe and cheer and do lots of praying. I know, now, that's been my calling all along—to help shape my kids in a way that will allow them to be flexible in God's hands. After all, a world is waiting.

Chapter 16

Self-Served
on a Silver Tray

This morning before John left for work, we snuggled on the living room couch and we prayed. His mouth was close to my ear, his warm breath soft on my cheek. It's one of my favorite things that we do together. Even if John's running out the door or I have a huge list of things I need to get started on for the day, it just feels right to pause and spend three quick minutes in prayer together.

It often feels as if we're just repeating the same words over and over, each day's requests the same. John prays for me, for the projects I'm working on, for the challenges I'm facing, and he prays for the kids. I pray for John's work, for God's wisdom and strength in his life, and for safety as he travels to the office. I also pray for the kids and Grandma and that I will be attentive to the needs of those around me.

Sometimes we add prayers for urgent needs, like troubles plaguing extended family members, or prayers for our church, our country, our world. We've prayed for people we know to accept Christ, and we pray that our home will be a place where people can feel God.

If anything, our prayer time is simple. And I think it's the simplicity that makes it work. We may not speak with eloquent phrases or pray page-long Scripture passages, but it's enough for us to pray in this simple way, in each other's arms. It's a reminder that God is with us through our day. It's a request for Him to release His provision and power into our ordinary circumstances. It's a plea for God to enter into our world and focus our thoughts.

Sometimes the kids walk in on us as we're praying (especially when there is no milk for cereal and they aren't sure how to survive!), but I think seeing us in that vulnerable place is okay. They like to see us together. They like to hear us lifting up our prayers to God, even if we're praying for them.

Especially if we're praying for them. Seeing us pray helps them know that prayer works.

When I was in the fifth grade, a friend stayed the night. Before we drifted off to sleep, Heidi climbed out of the bed, got on her knees, and prayed. At the time, prayer wasn't a part of my nightly ritual. But seeing her there, it hit me that something wasn't right. If God is God, then couldn't He hear my prayers as I lay on my bed? Didn't my whispered requests meet His ears, no matter what position I was in?

I remember another time I prayed in the second grade for something I wanted. It was a book of Barbie paper dolls. You know—the kind with the perforated edges and all those cool two-dimensional clothes to dress that cardboard figure in.

I desperately wanted the paper doll book, so I prayed. I told God He could make it appear, and I'd keep it just between me and Him. I made a deal, and I told Him He could drop it in my closet, and I'd only play with it when my mom wasn't around. I prayed so hard and so long (for a second grader) that I was highly disappointed the next day when I opened the closet door and the paper doll book wasn't there.

Disappointment trailed me for a week, until I was certain that God wasn't all people talked Him up to be. Until…my birthday arrived. And guess what I received? The paper doll book! It's wasn't my only gift, but it's the only one I remember today. It struck me then as I pondered it with all the contemplation a seven-year-old possessed, that God had answered my prayer after all, just not in the way I expected.

I always felt like a prayer failure. I can't count the number of prayer journals I've started in which I dutifully listed all the prayer needs that entered my mind. I'd listed my husband, kids, friends, grandparents, cousins, aunts, parents, friends of friends and all the associated needs. The only problem was it was easier to list them than actually pray for them. Sometimes I'd get through a few requests before time ran out. Worse yet were the weeks and months when I neglected the list. Guilt plagued me. God needed people of prayer, and I didn't fit the bill. Not only that; I wasn't even taking my place in the audience of those who wanted to see Him at work.

It was my kids who got me questioning how prayer worked. They wondered if there was a system. They wanted to know what way worked best when it came to bringing our prayers to God.

I remember once when they were all staying over at a friend's house. With five kids who needed to say their bedtime prayers, my friend Twyla told them, "Tonight we're going to do 'popcorn prayers.' Everyone pray one sentence, starting from the youngest and moving to the oldest."

Twyla and the kids closed their eyes and waited for my son Nathan, the youngest, to begin. When he didn't start after twenty seconds, Twyla opened her eyes and noticed Nathan raising his hand.

"Uh, Mrs. Klundt, I forgot the rules."

There are, of course, no rules to prayer. Unless you count that you must believe to receive. There are times I say I believe, but my actions prove otherwise. Like the weeks before a missions trip when we were still many thousands of dollars short. I was talking to the others about ways we could cut costs when Nathan interrupted.

"Mom, I don't know what you're stressing about. I prayed about it, and I have peace that all the money will come in. After all, it was God who told us to go."

After that reminder, I had peace too. Nathan was right. It *was* God who told us to go. It wasn't the first time I had to be reminded.

———

Fourteen years ago my husband and I made the biggest move of our lives. We were a young married couple with three kids, five and under, and we felt God calling us to move to Montana. It didn't matter that we hadn't been there before. It didn't matter that John didn't have a job or that we didn't have a permanent place to stay. We wanted a quieter, slower-paced environment to raise our children other than busy California. Our friends who'd moved there claimed Montana was the Promised Land.

We wavered about the decision for a year and then pleaded, *Lord, if you want us to go, make it clear to us. We need money to move and enough to live on for a few months until we can find work.*

God answered clearly.

At that time, John worked on commission selling computers. Usually he sold two computers a week, but John went to work the day after our prayer and had eleven sales, enough money to pay for our new, God-given adventure!

On our drive to Montana, we eagerly anticipated what God had in store for us. And we weren't disappointed. Three weeks after arriving, John had found a better job than the one he had in California. We bought our first house six months after that.

Looking back, it's now easy to see God's plan. It was the "before" part that took faith. Especially when not everyone believed we were making the right decision. My mother begged us not to go. "How are you going to provide for these three babies?" My husband's parents were sure we were moving to join a commune. (Not quite!)

It was hard when people challenged the decisions John and I were making. It also made me question if we were, indeed, following God's call. I questioned then, and I still do. After all, sometimes what God asks me to do is different from the way He seems to work with others. How come we're the ones He called to move a thousand miles away? How come I'm the one He directed to homeschool and help start a crisis pregnancy center? *Why me, Lord?*

Some people may accuse me of doing too much. Sometimes I agree with them. But then there is a part of me that wants to follow God—wholeheartedly, completely, and full throttle, wherever He may lead. I don't want to look back fifty years from now and think, *What if I had trusted God? Where would I be?*

Yet there are other times I wonder if I jump on the bandwagon just because something seems like a good idea...or because I'm capable. I took the position of volunteer regional director for a mothering organization because of that. I resigned only after I realized I hated paperwork and would rather work with women than manage them. Just because there is a need and I am a warm body, that doesn't mean it's a fit.

That's where prayer comes in. It's taking everything before God and listening for His voice. It's asking that my heart reflect His heart. It's begging for discernment and reading His Word. It's not depending on popcorn prayers to get you through. Instead, it's looking back at what God has done and considering what direction He is providing. And then it's stepping out in trust that God will pull you back if He needs to.

I don't ask myself, *What things do I need to finish today?*

I pray, *God, what would you have me do?*

I don't worry about all that needs to get done (or at least I try not to). I just ask God, *What's next?*

Sometimes God directs me to take one of my kids out to lunch, tidy my desk, call a friend, or have lunch with a teen mom.

On more than one occasion, I've prayed about my tasks and felt God saying, *Don't stress out, but* none *of those things will get done today.* And sure enough, a friend needs a ride to the doctor, a child is sick, or my car gets a flat tire—things that would have stressed me out before I began to ask God to direct my life and my days.

The key (one I'm reminding myself about even now) is not seeing such things as unexpected, out-of-the-blue requests, but rather as opportunities to keep my ears open to the voice of the Spirit.

I don't know what the perfect balance is. For me, it changes daily. I don't have the right formula, and even if I did, I'm sure my formula wouldn't work for anyone else. Instead, I pray and ask God to guide me. Sometimes I listen and get it right. Other times, I forget to listen.

That's what happened just two days ago. I'd been traveling to attend a retreat, and my family was missing having me around. After I returned, Grandma was especially eager for us to spend some time together.

I'll take her out later in the week, I told myself. *I need to get a few things done first. Need to get caught up.*

I tried to keep the long to-do list out of my mind as I prayed about God's hand upon my day. But the list just hung around, like a stray puppy that wanted some attention, so I decided to pray for the things that plagued me. (What a concept!) I prayed that I'd get a lot accomplished and I'd be able to catch up on some of the things I was behind on. I prayed for success in my work so I could make time to take my grandmother to lunch.

A few minutes later, as I sat down at my desk and looked at the piles of waiting mail, waiting e-mails, and waiting work projects, something stirred within me. I realized that I'd been praying that God would help me to fulfill the things that I wanted to accomplish, but I'd forgotten to ask what He had in store for my day.

God turned my thoughts to my sweet grandmother, and I considered how hard it must be to be seventy-nine years old and unable to get out and drive oneself around. He reminded me that not very many people my age have grandmas around, let alone grandmas who live with them. How many of my friends would love to have their grandma back for just one day, for just one lunch?

Logic told me that I needed to work. There were people expecting to hear from me, yet my heart told me those things could wait. Feeling God's urging, I hurried downstairs and asked Grandma if she'd like to go to lunch. Her face lit up.

"Really?"

"Yep. Go put on your lipstick and earrings, and we'll go out to eat, and then I'll take you shopping."

"Oh good," my grandma said. "I've been making a list, but I know you are busy. I think God heard my prayers."

I just nodded and smiled, knowing He had.

I'd like to say that I went to lunch and didn't think about the to-do lists or the piles on my desk. That wasn't the case. I had to force myself not to check e-mail on my cell phone as I waited for Grandma to finish her soup and sandwich. (She claims I eat too fast. I insist she eats too slow.) I also had to calm myself as I stood at the end of the grocery checkout line for thirty minutes as Grandma finished shopping.

It's okay. God knows, I told myself. *He's aware of the list…Everything will get done when it needs to get done.*

So I waited and I smiled, and as I stood there it was almost as if God was telling me, *Doing what I ask you to do is more important than anything else. Waiting at the store is even more important than finishing a big work project if you're doing what I ask.*

When Grandma finished shopping and we returned home, that same peace stayed with me as I set to work on the piles. By the time dinner rolled around, I looked over my list and realized that I had gotten more done than I'd anticipated, even with the lunch date and shopping trip thrown in.

As I prayed that night, I thanked God for the realization that He can help me achieve more than I could ever do on my own. God can do more with less time. He can expand my ability when I live my life in obedience.

In the end, it comes down to me taking my days, my hours, and my minutes before God and holding them up to Him as a servant would hold up a silver tray to her master. *Here you go, Lord. Order this. Make sense of this. I lay it all before you.* It's asking for priorities and for the power to do them. It's asking for peace that I am where He wants me to be. Then I depend on Him, on His strength, on His wisdom to do what He puts before me.

Sometimes these things don't make sense, like ignoring my work deadline to reach out to a friend or adding a missions trip or a foreign exchange student in our already busy lives. But I trust that God has the bigger picture in mind. And when I'm stretched beyond what I can manage on my own, that's the place I need to be. That's when I need to need Him.

There's no other place I'd rather be.

Chapter 17

Then Stings My Soul

The phone rang, and I checked the caller ID. It was the police department. I put the cordless phone back into the holder.

I get calls from them once a year, asking for donations for D.A.R.E., the Drug Abuse Resistance Education program, or something similar. I usually give, but that day I was more focused on getting some work done. John was out of town, and the younger kids were with friends. Cory was working, which meant I had a few hours to check off some of the things on my to-do list.

Ten seconds after the ringing stopped, it started again. The caller ID again said it was the police department. Someone really wanted to get through to me. My heart began to pound.

"Hello?"

"Is this Tricia Goyer?" The voice sounded official.

"Yes…"

"We have your son Cory here. We need you to come down."

"Come down?"

"To the police station."

"I don't understand. Cory is at work."

"Cory *was* at work. He's in our custody now. The store manager called and had us come and arrest him. We can explain more when you get here."

Arrest him?

I don't remember if I responded after that. Or what I did. I hardly remember getting myself in the car and driving down to the police station.

I do remember the look on Cory's face as I walked into the holding room. His eyes were filled with sadness, mixed with pain, mixed with regret. I understood the phrase "he had guilt written all over his face" even better. I swallowed hard and turned my attention to the officer.

"What's going on, Officer?" I dared to ask.

"It seems that yesterday a customer purchased a gift card and then forgot it at the check stand. Sometime later Cory found it. Instead of turning it in, he used it to purchase a few video games. When the people came back for their gift card, they found it had already been used. That's when the store discovered Cory's part."

I glanced again at Cory's face, and I knew without a doubt what the officer was saying was true. Cory's eyes teared up, and he looked down at his lap.

I wanted to argue with the officer. I wanted to ask Cory, "WHAT WERE YOU THINKING?" I wanted to wake up from this bad dream. I wanted this to be a misunderstanding. Instead, I took a deep breath and realized that even though I never expected something like this to happen, it was happening, and I was the adult. I had to help my son deal with the consequences.

"Okay, so what happens now?"

"Well, when I questioned Cory, he admitted what he did," the officer continued. Then I saw the officer's face soften. "He's not like most of the kids I see in here. They try to deny it, get out of it, or blame someone else. You've got a good kid here who made a stupid mistake. Cory's promised me he's not going to do anything else like this again."

Well, at least my son's an honest thief. I tried to take comfort in that fact.

"Yes…" I couldn't get out more than one word, and I couldn't look at Cory because I felt certain my heart would break if I did.

"I'll release him to you, but you need to make an appointment tomorrow to visit juvenile services. They'll figure out a plan for restitution."

"Okay, and what do you think that will include?"

"Most likely community service and possibly peer court."

"Sure. That makes sense."

The officer handed me the papers that I needed to sign for my son's release. Less than ten minutes after walking into the police station, I walked out with my son.

"Sorry, Mom," Cory said once we got into the car. His voice quivered.

"I forgive you, Cory, just like God will forgive you if you ask. I still love you, you know." Emotion caught in my voice, and Cory nodded.

I started the car and pulled out of the parking spot.

"So they walked you out of the store in handcuffs?" My gut ached thinking about it.

"Yep."

"I bet that was hard."

"Very."

My chest tightened as I pictured the scene in my mind's eye. Everyone watching the police officer walking Cory out. Everyone gawking. My heart hurt.

"I bet it was the worst thing you've ever faced," I said, driving him back home.

"No. The worst thing was when the officer called you. When you found out."

I couldn't speak after that. Not a word.

The drive home was one of the hardest I've ever made. On the way, I called John and asked him to cut his trip short. I needed him. I needed help.

Various emotions surged through me as my mind wrapped around the choice Cory had made. Sadness that he'd done what he'd done. Embarrassment—for him and our family—as I realized it was possible that people we knew had seen the arrest. And even thankfulness that Cory had been caught. He'd chosen wrongly, and he needed to face the consequences. Worse would have been if he'd gotten away with it. What then?

But more than anything, my heart ached because life was hard. There was no smooth road. I couldn't make every decision for my son. I couldn't stop him from making bad ones.

I also mourned because Cory's innocence had been destroyed…by his own hand. A desire for something he could obtain easily had won over his knowledge of what was right. I knew what those longings were like. I'd faced them myself and hadn't always chosen well.

We arrived home, and Cory and I sat for a while in silence. Both of us were lost in our thoughts, and as I looked at my son, I realized that the love between us was still strong. Maybe even stronger than the hour before the phone call. I silently prayed that this experience would draw him closer to God. I prayed that from this he would realize that he could not face life depending on his own strength.

The hard stuff isn't easy. And seeing God mold our kids often hurts even more than feeling His hand on us. But it's also through the hard stuff that we see God in different ways. We discover an element of His goodness that had before been unknown. Undiscovered.

―――

I held my four-month-old baby on my lap and felt both embarrassed and angry. But mostly I was worried. Very worried.

"You have a very sick baby here." The nurse held out her arms, wanting me to pass Cory over. "The doctor needs to get fluid into him as quickly as possible. Why did you wait so long to bring him in?" Her tone had more than a hint of accusation.

"I didn't wait. I took him to the clinic two days ago. The doctor said it was just colic."

"A 103-degree fever is not colic," she snapped, taking Cory from my arms. "Please wait outside… We'll let you know…"

Ever since my son's birth, I'd been treated more like his baby-sitter than his mother. Four months earlier when I'd been released from the hospital, the nurse had explained the paperwork to *my* mother, as if I was too stupid to understand what she was saying.

I was angry because I'd known two days earlier that something was wrong and I'd taken Cory to the doctor. I knew it. Cory wasn't eating right. He was crying a lot. He had a slight fever at the time.

Now I was worried because the doctors had discovered what was wrong—spinal meningitis. It didn't matter how Cory got it; the problem was he had it. And he was sick.

I waited outside the curtained-off section with my mom and our pastor's wife, Darlyne. I wrapped my arms around myself, but my hands wouldn't stop trembling. Darlyne prayed beside me.

Please God. Please help Cory. Heal him. I repeated those words over and over.

I could hear the doctors and nurses talking. They couldn't find a vein for the IV.

"Get a shunt. It's the only way I know to get fluid into him," the doctor demanded.

One nurse scurried out of the room. The other came out to tell us what was happening.

"He's too dehydrated. We can't get a needle into his veins. The doctor's going to put a shunt directly into his leg bone to get fluids into him. Then we're going to fly him down to the nearest children's hospital. Tricia, you'll be flying with him."

I nodded as tears filled my eyes. The anger and the embarrassment were gone. The worry grew. I just wanted my son to be okay.

My mom discussed plans to bring me my things. She would drive down.

A few minutes later, amidst Cory's screams of pain, we received good news that the shunt had worked. Before I could grasp what was happening, I was sitting in a small airplane with two nurses. The thirty-minute ride was silent. The nurses didn't speak. Neither did I. But I did pray. With everything in me, I prayed my son would be okay.

I don't remember much for the next few days. I remember I slept in a hospital bed next to Cory's hospital crib. I remember not being able to hold him. I remember how limp he looked. How sick. I remember walking around, up and down the halls, seeing very sick kids and very weary and worried parents in every room. Other babies like Cory were there, and bigger kids with serious health problems. I remember thinking,

When you have a child, you never think of this. This isn't what you signed up for.

But peering into Cory's crib, I knew that I'd go through all the pain and heartache again if I had to. He was worth it. Having him was worth it. I didn't want to lose him. I couldn't imagine that. Instead of making me regret I'd ever become a mother, the pain and the worry made me realize the intensity of my love. Increased it.

Four days after Cory was admitted, he was released. The doctors called his quick recovery a miracle, and I agreed. God had healed my son. He'd also touched me. For the first time I discovered that, even in the hard stuff of mothering, God was there. And maybe He was even closer than before because I needed Him more.

I have a feeling God knows how much these kids mean to us. And because of that He also knows that when there is pain in their lives, He'll get our attention.

My heart aches when I read the plea of the father in Matthew 17:15, " 'Lord, have mercy on my son,' he said. 'He has seizures and is suffering greatly. He often falls into the fire or into the water.' "

Reading that verse, I wonder if the man would have sought out Jesus if his son would have been well. Would he have made time in his day to seek the Teacher if life had been happy? But it wasn't happy. His son was hurting and in trouble. The father went to Jesus, pleaded with Him, because his heart ached.

*Have mercy…*we pray when we have a sick child. *Have mercy…*we pray through every hard circumstance, even the ones our children have chosen for themselves.

And God did. God showed mercy by sending His Son. And it's because of Jesus that I've discovered hope for my children.

As a Father, God knew joy: "And a voice from heaven said, 'This is my Son, whom I love; with him I am well pleased'" (Matthew 3:17).

God also knew pain.

"At that moment the curtain of the temple was torn in two from top to bottom. The earth shook and the rocks split.…When the centurion and those with him who were guarding Jesus saw the earthquake and all that had happened, they were terrified, and exclaimed, 'Surely he was the Son of God!'" (Matthew 27:51, 54).

The more I think about it, the more I understand God's love and sacrifice when I see God acting in my children's lives. It's the hard stuff of life—the pulling and tugging of our hearts—that best shapes our understanding of God's love, even if we wish it were not so.

It was difficult seeing the pain Cory went through as a baby. I hated watching Cory face the hard consequences of his poor choice. But in both places I understood God better. As Cory worked off his community service and went through a trial in peer court, he learned a few things too—that God loves us even in the hard stuff and that his parents still love him too.

But I don't think Cory will fully understand until he has kids of his own. We always say, "Just wait until you have kids," and we should. It's then that all of us learn how much God is present in the heartache of a parent's heart.

Chapter 18

Start with My Heart

I wish I'd known the truth sooner about Leslie's friendship with Candace. Candace is the daughter of one of our good friends. Since we spent a lot of time with her parents, my daughter spent a lot of time with her. I never suspected anything was wrong. Leslie and Candace were around the same age, and they played together well. It wasn't until just a few months ago, when Leslie was sixteen, that I realized how much my daughter had suffered because of things Candace had said.

I was working on a project with a wonderful young woman, Kristen, who survived a suicide attempt. One day as Leslie and I were driving around doing errands, I started telling her about Kristen's story.

"That will be a really good book, Mom, because there are a lot of kids and teens who need to know suicide is not the answer." Leslie was quiet for a moment. Then she continued, "You know, I've even considered suicide before."

Her words hit my heart and then sank as if they were filled with concrete.

"What? Are you serious?" The whispered words escaped my lips, and I glanced over at her.

"I would have never done it, but it crossed my mind."

"Why?" My mind rewound through Leslie's life, trying to pick out any traumatic moments that could have led to these thoughts.

"Well," Leslie seemed hesitant to answer. "It was because of Candace. Every time we got together, she told me how worthless I was."

"She did?"

"Yeah. All the time."

"What did she tell you?" My hands gripped the steering wheel tighter.

"She told me that she was prettier and that I would never have a boyfriend. She told me I was dumb because I was home-schooled and that she was better at sports. She told me that I didn't have any friends and she had lots." The words spilled out of Leslie's mouth.

"And you believed her?" I touched my daughter's arm.

Leslie shrugged. "Yeah. I thought she was my best friend. We were always together. I thought she was right. She *was* better at sports. She did have lots of friends at school."

"Maybe, but you are beautiful…and smart, too. Didn't you know that? Didn't Dad and I let you know how much we love you and how wonderful you are?"

Leslie shrugged. "Yeah, but I thought you were just saying that because you were my mom. I thought you *had* to say those things."

"Do you still feel that way? Do you still struggle with those thoughts?"

"No, not at all. I'm closer with God now. I know how much He loves me, but for a few years, life was really hard."

I walked through the rest of the day as if I was only half-awake. One part of me felt dead inside. I hated knowing that Leslie had been going through so much pain and that I'd been clueless. I also hated knowing that perhaps some of her issues had occurred because she'd been watching me. For many years I struggled with comparing my weaknesses with other people's strengths. For many years I struggled with feeling like I couldn't compare with those around me.

Tara and I came close to never becoming friends. I met her a couple of months after her husband started working with mine, but her reputation preceded her. While I was happy to get a prepackaged meal on the table, I heard that Tara cooked culinary delights, complete with homemade desserts. My idea of canned vegetables consisted of those I picked up from the grocery-store shelf, but it was rumored that Tara's shelves were lined with jars of produce she grew and canned herself. She also sewed her children's quilts and stamped all her own greeting cards. I was intimidated, to say the least.

So the first time we met was less than a success. Tara was nice, but reserved. I was no better. The reason for her lack of warmth, I found out later, was that she was equally intimidated by what she had heard about me. I was a writer who home-schooled my children and led children's church week after week. Tara felt she could never live up to my accomplishments, and I was sure I fell far below hers.

Then we got to know each other.

One morning, although no audible voice echoed from the sky, I felt God leading me to invite Tara and her family over for dinner. I asked John to make the arrangements and then set to work on my best recipe. (I later remembered that I had served the same meal to her husband only a few months before!) When Tara called to confirm the invitation, she offered to bring dessert. I told her not to bother, but she insisted, confessing that she had more than a dozen homemade pies stored in her freezer. *A dozen?* How could I say no?

Dinner turned out well, but the conversation afterward was the turning point. As Tara and I strolled in the woods behind my house, she asked me about church. As I shared my family's testimony, her face glowed with excitement. Before the evening was out, Tara and her husband had made plans to join a Bible study with us the following week. Soon they were regularly attending worship service, and both rededicated their lives to God. A few months later they were baptized.

I don't know how long it was after our friendship started that the confessions of our initial misgivings came out. We'd both been so busy comparing our weaknesses to each other's strengths that we had successfully held each other at bay for over a year. Yet as time passed, I realized my feeling of intimidation had transformed to appreciation. Instead of feeling inferior, I asked Tara to teach me how to make jelly and bake a pie from scratch. I, in turn, encouraged her growth in God and provided a listening ear for her struggles with her husband and kids. She, too, had decided to homeschool her children and wanted my advice. She even started helping out with children's church. Instead of putting us at odds, our differences became a point of bonding.

While our friendship continued to blossom, I longed for a way to show my appreciation. It was then that I thought of the jar.

One morning, I took a small canning jar and some strips of paper, and then I sat down to write. On each piece of paper, I wrote one thing that I appreciated about Tara.

I appreciate your creativity. Many people benefit from your small, special touches.

I appreciate your availability to others. You are always there to listen and to care.

I appreciate how you help out when I need it. I love knowing you're only a phone call away.

I appreciate how you invite my kids into your home and enjoy having them around.

By the time I finished, thirty slips of paper were filled out, one for each day of the month.

How close Tara and I were to missing each other completely! And how sad that my daughter struggled with the same thing—this horrible feeling of not measuring up.

———

One day as I was talking to my daughter about God and life, I had this impression. *What I do for God is great, but perhaps my work is just a stepping stone for what He is going to do through my kids.* It's both humbling and encouraging to know the work God started in me can continue, and perhaps grow, through Cory, Leslie, and Nathan.

Yet I've also learned that the struggles I have are sometimes magnified in the lives of my kids. All those years when I mumbled about someone else being better, smarter, prettier, or more organized, my kids were tuning in. They were spectators in my three-ring-circus act of having everything "just so"—the house, the kids, my work, my life.

The truth is, the saying, "Do what I say, not what I do," never works. I see my angst lived out most in Cory (who was older and the most observant during my I-just-want-everything-perfect stage of life). He is the one who walks around the house straightening up the coats and shoes. He's the one who notices anything that's misplaced. He washes his face after every meal and is particular about his hair. He's the one who, within ten seconds of walking into his room, knows if someone's been in there and what was touched. I hate the fact that this is something I've passed on. I also dislike seeing that when things don't turn out as Cory perfectly planned, he has a tendency to shut down. Whether it's about a video he's wanting to shoot or a youth event he's wanting to teach at, he has a habit of slinking off and turning it over to someone else instead of trying to figure out how to fix what's broken. It's my struggle only tweaked and intensified. Poor kid.

Seeing this makes me want to work on my issues. It makes me want to ignore the little voice that tells me, "It's no big deal," and instead try to change—or rather turn to God who has the power to help me change. I'm constantly going to God and telling Him, *Here you go. Take this tendency in me to compare. Or this natural habit to pick out everything that's wrong. I can't handle it anymore. I surrender to you. Form me as you desire. Change me.*

But it's not only surrender that makes the difference. It's also being willing to do the things God asks me to do, like call Tara. To step out of my comfort zone and be willing to let God use me as He forms me. Or to understand that perhaps the forming firms up through use.

When my kids, and someday grandkids and great-grandkids, look back, I'd like them to see me as a solid stone that helped build our family on a strong foundation rather than on a pool of quicksand that sucked everyone else down. As Psalm 89:1 says, "I will sing of the LORD's great love forever; with my mouth I will make your faithfulness known through all generations." That's what I desire—for my song of faithfulness to continue long after I'm gone.

Chapter 19

The Songs
I Once Resisted

I sit at my desk, breathing in the fresh spring air coming through the cracked-open window and humming along to "Eye of the Tiger" by Survivor. It's my son who's really listening to it. He likes that song, which surprises me. I remember dancing to it at an eighth grade dance. The gym/cafeteria was dim, and despite the fact that my body, emotions, and crushes were under a constant state of awkward change, I danced with carefree abandon. Or at least I pretended to. In reality, I wondered if I had the right moves, and I wondered if the boy who smiled at me from across the dance floor that night would acknowledge me the next day. My son, of course, can't understand the memories that flash through my thoughts as the song plays—like the photos clicking through a red, plastic View-Master. The song feeds the images.

Me with my permed hair. *Click.*

Me sitting on the top of the cafeteria table and wondering if Jason A. liked my permed hair. *Click.*

Me feeling the beat of "Eye of the Tiger" and swinging my permed hair as I danced. *Click.*

My son doesn't realize any of this, and he wouldn't understand even if I tried to explain. He sees Mom. The mom who, when he was a toddler, held a washcloth to his forehead as I rinsed his hair, making sure the soap didn't get in his eyes. The mom who sat in the Big Bird beanbag chair, reading him storybooks—*Button Soup* and *Robin Hood* being top picks. The mom who cheered at all the soccer and basketball games. And who was the first to tie his shoes and sign his cast.

What my son also doesn't know is that the awkwardness of that eighth-grade Madonna wannabe didn't go away like my hairstyle did. The truth is, being a mom brought with it a level of intensity to match the intensity of those junior high days. From the moment the two pink lines on the pregnancy test told me I was expecting, my body and emotions have been in a constant, awkward state of change.

The only difference is that unlike a junior high crush, my love for my son doesn't fade. And when two more kids were added to the equation, the love only multiplied.

My love as a mom is the real deal. And that's what makes the mommy View-Master images matter so much more.

Me standing around with the other preschool moms, hiding my tears as I leave Cory in a teacher's care for the first time. *Click.*

Me having to apologize to my son for losing my temper… again. *Click*.

Me having to watch my oldest drive off alone in a car for the first time. *Click*.

I may have looked like I knew what I was doing—that I was cool with my son's growing and changing—but many times I felt as phony as Milli Vanilli.

I have three kids. Two are polar opposites, and one is in the middle. My poles are Leslie—gregarious, academic (although only when I make her), vocal, and friendly to everyone she meets but confrontational on issues she's serious about. Then there is Nathan. Twenty-two months younger, he's introspective, smart but unmotivated, nonverbal (think battleship sounds rather than actual words), a dedicated friend.

If these two didn't come out of my womb, I'd think they came from two different planets. They've been unique from age one when their personalities started shining through. Cory— my oldest—is a mix of both, more quiet than outgoing but also friendly and loving. He's a daredevil, breaking the ice to jump into the lake (which happened earlier this year). Climbing a cliff and calling to his parents far below. (Did I mention the climbing incident happened when he was three?)

It was a beautiful day on the California coast—slightly cloudy but warm. A day full of promise.

We vacationed with a group of our friends, renting a huge house on the beach. We'd shared pancakes and laughter all morning, and then we went off to explore. Leslie, just a baby, was in a front pack.

I probably paid more attention to the colored seashells nestled in moist sand than I did to my son. I thought John was watching him; John thought I was.

"Hi, Mom!" The words came from above me, but I immediately knew the voice.

"Cory?" I glanced around and then up. Way up. A group of men were attempting to scale a boulder/mountain, and Cory peered down at them from the peak. He waved at me from the edge.

"Cory, how did you get up there?" My heart pounded in my chest. My throat tightened, and I didn't know what to say. Didn't know what to do.

Cory pointed behind him to another trail, easier than the one the others had found.

"Cory, sit!" John's voice was firm. "Sit and don't move. I'll be right up."

Mixed emotions flooded me. Fear. Worry. Pride. He was a boy, all right. All boy.

Cory sat. His dad raced to the top. A smile filled Cory's face until he saw the fear in his father's eyes. I held his hand for the rest of the day, not wanting to let go. But after that day Cory didn't stop climbing. It was in him from the first moment he could stand. It was part of his song.

Cory's unique melody came unexpectedly. Yet from the first cry after his birth, he sang it loud and clear. It's a song of independence and courage and deep love and some timidity with anything new, with an underlying chord of gentleness that often surprises those who get to know him.

When I first had kids, I believed I had more control of the melody. Yet even though Cory is now taller than me, I can sometimes see the bold, independent, devoted toddler peeking out through his eyes. He lives life according to the melody placed inside him before birth—one I realize now that I had no part of.

When my kids were younger, I used to think of them more like empty vessels. I was the mom, and I believed it was my job to fill them up with all the good things of life—things to make them well rounded and—let's face it—better than any other kid who's ever been born.

I signed them up for sports, for music, for dance, because there was a lot to instill in these few, soon-to-pass child years. But no matter what activity I shuffled them around to, my kids played their own song. They acted in ways that I was all too familiar with at home but that I hoped would suddenly change in public.

And instead of humming along with their uniqueness, I was embarrassed when Cory wasn't aggressive in basketball or when Leslie cared more for the costume than the dance steps or when Nathan introduced himself as "nincompoop" during his first day of soccer, which brought lots of laughs. I wanted them to be the model children I'd formed in my head—the brilliant, athletic, witty, and artistic ones that reside in the gray matter of every pregnant woman.

It wasn't until years later, after we'd attempted T-ball, dance, tumbling, Spanish, art, soccer, choir, and swimming with minimal success, that I realized one of my biggest struggles had to do more with me than with my kids. I wanted them to shine because that would reflect well on me. Inside, I still felt like that junior high, permed-hair girl who worried about what others thought. The one who appeared to be enjoying herself but inwardly was fretting. The one who longed for the boldness, who danced to "Eye of the Tiger" but was unsure of her steps. I wanted my kids to be good so I would look great. If I had the kid who won at everything, then maybe I'd feel valued as a mom.

It makes me sad now to realize all the time I wasted trying to make my kids look good so I could look good, especially when God placed a unique stamp on each of their souls and called them good from the beginning.

It helps now that my kids are older. Their songs are more distinct, and the chords I often fought are now the ones I applaud.

Leslie's strong-willed nature has helped her stand firm against teen temptations. She is the one who lectures her friends about purity and is the first to introduce herself in a crowd.

Cory's caring yet tenacious attitude carried him when a knee injury halted his basketball playing just weeks before the state tournament. And spoke through him as he cheered his team on.

Nathan's ease at being a friend helps him reach out to others who don't feel as if they fit in. And his jokes and playfulness break up the tension in new situations.

I only wish I could have known this before. To realize my children's Creator knew *them* from the beginning. King David knew this. Psalm 139 is one of my favorites. In it David sings about God creating us and knowing us, forming our bones and preparing our days. It's silly to think that God didn't make my kids right. Or that He missed an important element (like artistic genius and athletic aptitude) when forming them. Even though they may be different than I expected, their designs were well thought out and beautiful.

There are still things I would like to change in my kids, through either subtraction or addition. I know that just as I've grown and changed with God, they will too. Doesn't the Bible say that God makes everything beautiful in its time?

Understanding this earlier would have helped save me time and energy as I attempted to form my kids into something they're not. Maybe I would have felt better about myself, too, as a mom. I would have danced a little more carefree, and with a little more abandon, realizing there are no perfect steps. Realizing that different is beautiful.

Realizing that God's song is not what I expected.

It's better.

Chapter 20

When Death Stopped at Our House

It wasn't until death came into our home that I became hungry for heaven.

Years ago, when we first talked about moving away from California, I had only one hesitation. "I know God is calling us to Montana. We've seen how He's provided the money—how He's provided everything—but I'm afraid," I confessed to John as we drove home from visiting my grandparents.

"Of what?" John reached over and took my hand.

"Of getting a phone call one day and having someone tell me that my grandma…or grandpa…is gone. That they died, and I missed the last years with them."

So when the call came, and I heard my mother's sniffly voice on the other end, my worry about losing one of my grandparents flashed through my mind. "Mom, is that you? What's wrong?"

"Tricia, there's something I need to tell you. It's about Grandpa."

I leaned against the kitchen counter, as if knowing I'd need something to hold me up. She sniffled again, and I sat on the bar stool.

"What is it?"

"Grandpa has a tumor on his bladder. They just discovered it. He's going to have laser surgery to remove it."

"Is it cancer?" The word lodged in my throat.

"The doctors are unsure if it is cancerous, but any surgery at his age is risky."

"When is the surgery?"

My mom filled me in on the details, and then she told me she'd let me know if she heard anything else.

Grandpa came through that surgery okay, but then he took a turn for the worse. The surgeon suggested more surgery, but Grandpa wasn't interested. He told us he'd lived a long life and wanted to enjoy whatever time he had left. That's when he agreed to take us up on our offer to live with us. So over Christmas break, my husband and I drove through a blizzard, packed my grandparents up, and moved them into our home.

At first Grandpa seemed fine. Sure, he was a little slower than normal, but that was to be expected. Every morning, I made my grandpa coffee and breakfast, then I homeschooled the kids and spent the afternoon talking with Grandpa. We talked about his growing up years on a farm in Kansas with his ten brothers and sisters. We talked about how he met Grandma. It was after World War II, and she was a waitress. After his work at the mill, he'd stop in for dinner at the café where she worked.

But as the weeks passed, Grandpa became weaker, and I started thinking about our eternal home. I listened to songs about heaven and read snippets from the Bible. I discovered when you're in that situation, lyrics and snippets are about as filling to your soul as reading a cookbook or watching a cooking show when you're hungry. It just makes you want the real thing.

Never having lost a close family member before, I had a hundred ideas of how I'd deal with death—fear, dread, horror—but none of them were right.

Four months after coming to live with us, my grandfather was bedridden. My grandmother and I would spend time in his room reading Scripture verses and praying with him. Then one day as the kids and I were getting ready to start the school day, my grandma called, "Tricia, I need you!"

Terrified, I raced down the stairs and into my grandparents' bedroom. A typically quiet man, my grandpa's hands were lifted. He was weeping like a baby. "Oh dear Jesus. Oh dear Jesus. I love you, dear Lord Jesus!" The words spilled from his lips.

At first I thought he was in pain or that he was breaking down because of his lack of strength. My grandma's hands were on his legs. She was praying with him. I joined her.

Tears streamed down my grandfather's face. I handed him a tissue.

He held it over his eyes, but the tears didn't stop. "I love you, dear Jesus. Thank you, dear Jesus." Five minutes, ten minutes passed. The prayers were the same.

Finally, he lifted the tissue away. "See those trees out the window?" He pointed outside. "They turned into a cross, and I saw Jesus reaching his hands out to me."

The tears returned. Tears of joy. Goose bumps prickled my skin, and I was sure heaven was touching down in the room. I was almost afraid to look up, so sure was I that I would see heaven's gates.

"I haven't seen anything like that ever," my grandpa said. "It's a miracle."

I agreed. "A miracle and a gift," I whispered.

A little while later as my grandpa slept, I asked my grandma exactly what happened.

"Grandpa was just sitting there, looking out the window. Then he started pointing. 'Look at that, Grandma,' he said. 'If I were an artist, I would love to paint that. Look at those white doves. Look at that lion. Oh, I'd love to paint that lion.'" Tears ran down my grandma's cheeks as she related the story to me.

"And then he just started praising God, crying, and lifting his hands. That must be when he saw Jesus." She smiled. "And that's when I called for you."

My heart was bursting with love for God and with thanksgiving for heaven. I didn't want to leave the bedroom, so certain was I that it had become holy ground.

The next day my grandfather went into a coma, and while I should have been terribly sad, my heart filled with peace. Every time I walked into the room, it seemed brighter and filled with the brush of angel wings, as if heaven had touched it.

Grandpa lasted five more days. During his last conscious moment he blew me a kiss. I knew what he was saying, "See you later, sweetheart." And I trust I will.

I know I'll meet him on the other side.

When we first invited Grandpa into our home, my biggest concern was how the children would handle his death. They had a hard enough time dealing with the dead bird in the backyard. How would they cope with the death of someone they loved very much?

When the hospice nurse, Peggy, started showing up more regularly, I knew the end was near. Grandpa began lying down more than sitting. He only stood to use the bathroom. After a while, he couldn't even do that.

Peggy was sweet and outgoing. She did her work with care and joy.

"I don't understand," I asked her one day. "How can you do this job?"

"Well, I've seen so many amazing things. I consider myself a delivery nurse, helping people make the journey into eternity."

The kids were good during the whole experience. I talked to them, and Peggy talked to them too. They spent as much time with their grandpa as possible. Their faith was so simple. They were excited Grandpa would soon be with Jesus.

Still, I took one day at a time, fearing the end. Fearing the moment I'd have to tell them that the great-grandpa they loved so much was gone. But even though Grandpa was sick and spent most of his day lying on the couch, my kids didn't treat him differently or awkwardly. And when he died, they wanted to give him one last kiss good-bye.

I entered the room first, and reality hit me. This was real. This was happening. I looked at my grandpa. He looked so thin, so frail; his chest neither rose nor fell. I opened the door wider. Cory, Leslie, and Nathan stood there. At ages ten, seven, and five, they seemed too young to have to face this. I ached for them more than I ached for myself.

"Are you sure you want to do this? Are you sure you want to come in?"

"Yes." Cory nodded, standing in the doorway.

"We have to say good-bye." Leslie added.

They entered quietly, and I noted the smallest hint of a smile on Nathan's face.

"Bye, Grandpa." Cory kissed his cheek.

"Say hi to Jesus for us," Leslie said.

Nathan was last, and he looked at me wide-eyed. "Grandpa is in heaven. That's so cool. I can't wait to go with him!"

After they exited, they jabbered the rest of the day about all the wonderful things Grandpa was experiencing. They talked about Grandpa seeing Jesus. About seeing other people he knew. About angels and about streets of gold. They knew enough about heaven to understand that it was an amazing place. And listening to them, I realized they got it…even more than I did. They understood what Psalm 116:15 says, "Precious in the sight of the LORD is the death of his saints." They were sad about losing their great-grandfather but excited by what he was experiencing. They were also filled with joy. They knew that because of Jesus they'd one day get to experience all that, too.

Death did come to our home, but it wasn't something my children feared. They trusted in the heaven we read about in Bible stories and in the celebration that would soon be happening in the sky. God wasn't just a figure in the sky. He was someone who would greet Grandpa at the pearly gates. Heaven wasn't a place of fluffy clouds, angels, and harps. It was a place where we'd forever be united with those we loved and cared for.

At funerals people talk about no more pain, suffering, tears. Preachers talk about eternity and love—as they should. But often they miss something. They forget the love story, like the love story between my grandfather and Jesus. Eternal life is knowing Him (see John 17:3), and that starts right here on earth. Seeing the tears on my Grandpa's face reminded me that the Hero had won. The one Jesus loves is His forever. And God isn't just a benefit of heaven. Heaven is all about Him.

During his lifetime, my grandpa loved the Lord in his own quiet way. He attended church every Sunday, and every morning he read from his big Bible, pausing to pray over each member of his family. He was a happy guy who loved helping others, and he rarely showed emotion. That's why seeing him in tears, lifting his hands in praise on his last conscious day, was so meaningful. Grandpa got a glimpse of heaven—of Jesus with His arms outstretched. And no matter how reserved Grandpa was in life, nothing could stop him from worshiping his Lord during his first glimpse of eternity.

While I'm not ready for my life to be over today, heaven has great appeal. I'll get to see what my grandpa saw forever. I'll get to smell what he smelled forever. I'll get to rejoice in the place of no tears, no pain forever. I'll get that first glimpse of my Savior's face. And then look into it…forever.

Chapter 21

Leading Where We Dream to Go

G lacier National Park is only forty-five minutes from our house. A half-day trip found us on the top of the Continental Divide. Wildflowers waved in the cold breeze as my family and I tromped along the trails near the top of Logan Pass. The cloud cover looked like icy fog, and a splattering of snowflakes fell. There wasn't anyplace I'd rather be than this place and with my family.

We walked around taking photos—of the mountains, of each other, of the contrast between the wildflowers and snow. And we told stories about other times we'd traveled up the mountains for a day away.

"Mom, remember that time we came up here with your veteran friend? It was snowing and Charlie collapsed, just fell straight back," Nathan said, pointing to the concrete stairs where Charlie had fallen.

"Ugh." My stomach ached with the memory. "How could I forget?"

"What happened?" asked Andrea, our foreign exchange student, who was enjoying her first day at the top of Logan Pass.

"We were hurrying to the visitor center, and it didn't cross my mind that Charlie was from Wisconsin—used to low altitude—and now we were at 6,600 feet," I explained.

"He was following me, and I turned around just in time to see him falling straight back."

"Oh no!" Andrea's eyes were wide.

My mind filled with the horror of seeing Charlie passed out on the ground. "My first thought was, *He survived World War II, and here I've gone and killed him on this hike!*"

I continued, "The paramedics checked him out, and he was fine, except for a bump on his head."

"He was so nice," Leslie added. "Mom, have you heard from Charlie lately?" she asked.

I updated her about Charlie and some of the other veterans we'd met over the years, and as I hiked around, gazing at the broad vistas, I considered how my children's horizons have been broadened by these amazing men.

I'd never thought twice about World War II. I saw myself as a mom who worked at home, writing about parenting. With three kids under ten, I had plenty to write about. Then came a trip to Europe with two friends. They were both novelists, researching for works in progress. I was still coming to terms with my grandfather's death from cancer. My husband decided that after juggling hospice visits, housecleaning, and kids' homework, a relaxing time with friends was just what I needed.

When my fellow travelers told me the final research stop was Mauthausen concentration camp in Austria, I thought that was the last thing I wanted to see. Why not stop by a museum in Vienna or attend a Mozart concert in the park? I'd witnessed death firsthand. I didn't need to hear about atrocities that took place decades ago.

But instead of giving us a tour of the camp, Martha—the camp historian—invited us into her home. She served us tea and biscuits. And then she started telling us stories.

"Near the end of the war, there was much confusion." Martha's thin hands spread jam on the flaky roll. "German guards knew both the Americans and Russians neared. Many officers fled. Of course, the approaching Americans had no idea what awaited them. Twenty-three GIs on reconnaissance came upon a camp filled with thin, skeletal men and women. They opened the gates, and 25,000 prisoners were liberated."

I thought about my grandfather. During his last days we'd discussed many things. He told me about growing up in Kansas with ten brothers and sisters during the Great Depression. He talked to me about moving to California from the

Dust Bowl. He'd mentioned the war only briefly, but I noted the pain in his eyes and quickly changed the subject. Yet as I sat listening to Martha, I wondered about those twenty-three men who had liberated the concentration camp. Were they still alive? Did horrific memories plague them? Did they realize that, even after all these years, a historian still shared *their* story?

My heart was full when we left Martha's home that day. It wasn't rest I had needed but a new passion. When I arrived home, I contacted the Eleventh Armored Division, which was the tank division the GIs had been a part of. I learned that eleven of the men were still alive, and I wrote a letter to each one, asking if I could interview them. Six veterans wrote back immediately, and they invited me to attend their reunion. They were excited that someone wanted to hear what they had to say, and more than anything I wanted to write their story.

Yet I also had concerns. How would I balance researching World War II, interviewing veterans, and writing a novel while homeschooling three kids? Would following my dream require sacrifices from my family?

I knew myself. I knew what happened when I got caught up in a project. The laundry didn't get done. I shooed the kids away, urging them to find something to entertain themselves. As I worked at my computer, the world around me became a distraction. Worse yet, a burden. I didn't want that to happen.

I talked to John about it.

"Well, if you're thinking about these things than it shows you're aware of them. It shows God is speaking to you," he said. "It just seems like God has given you this story, and you should do what it takes to see where this path leads."

I took John's advice and told the men I would come. A few months later, I traveled from Montana to Michigan to attend the fifty-ninth reunion of the Eleventh Armored Division. A friend traveled with me, and we both believed that it would take a couple of days for the veterans to get to know us, to warm up to us, to share their stories. To our surprise, dozens of men were already waiting to talk to us when we arrived. I later learned they'd been lined up for most of the day!

The first two men I spoke to were Arthur and Charlie. They shared stories about their battles. They talked about many funny incidents that happened in Europe. Then I started asking about the camp and the liberation. Voices quieted. Eyes lowered. Hands trembled as the two veterans revisited the place that was never far from their thoughts. Other veterans shared their personal experiences, and although they were old men, I saw the look of young heroes in their gazes.

When I arrived home, I shared the stories I'd heard with my husband and children. I showed them photos, and soon they became used to hearing from the men themselves.

"Mom, it's one of your old guys on the phone!" my children would call out. Then at dinner I'd share the new stories I'd heard.

I took the many, many recorded stories and used them as

the inspiration for my first novel. It took one and a half years to write. John and the kids celebrated as I received the first copy in the mail. We celebrated again when the German and Dutch versions arrived.

Yet my passion didn't stop with this one novel. I continued to write others from the stories I heard, and my children continued to be impacted.

One year I organized homeschoolers in our area to interview veterans. Over a dozen kids participated, including mine. Every week, two or three veterans visited our group. The junior high and high school students heard stories from veterans like Lester, who was in the fourth wave to hit the beach at Iwo Jima, and Alan, who was a bomber navigator over the South Pacific. Before these interviews, history to these kids meant dates and black and white photos, but now it was represented by real men with real stories.

Then there was that year when Charlie came from Wisconsin to visit our family. He'd been in one of the first units to care for the former camp prisoners at Mauthausen concentration camp. Charlie attended church with us. He shared his story not only with my family but also with my church family.

When I first started on this journey, I thought following my dream would take away from my family, but the truth is we've all received so much in return, including the relationships we have with dozens of men — many, many grandpas.

When I first had kids, I envisioned them as leaders. I saw them as kind and caring. I pictured people who would take time to listen and understand. And then, when they got older, I realized I needed to be those things in order for my kids to follow my example.

More than that, I can only lead others where I'm willing to go myself.

I didn't plan on connecting my kids to veterans, but their hearts turned to these wonderful men. I didn't set out to connect them to history, but history is alive in our home. A dozen or so veterans still write and e-mail us on a weekly basis. Many more have passed away. Yet it warms my heart to know these men died knowing their stories would live on. It warms my heart to know my children will always remember these heroes.

Even today I received a letter from my veteran friend Leroy. He wrote to tell me about his recent stroke and about a special woman he still corresponds with.

When Hana read my novel, she got in touch with me and asked me about the men I had interviewed. It "just so happened" that she told me about one special American medic who had saved her life at the end of World War II.

I asked Hana more about her story, and she told me she'd been born in one concentration camp and then had traveled to Mauthausen with her mother. She was just three weeks old and very close to death when the camp was liberated. Her body was covered with horrible sores from a skin infection, and she would have died had it not been for this kindhearted medic. He had taken a full day to lance, care for, and clean her wounds. Because of his attention, she survived, and now she's a doctor living in California.

When I heard Hana's story, I thought about Leroy, so I gave her his name and number. In their first conversation, Hana discovered Leroy was the man who'd saved her.

"I'd always wondered about you," Leroy said. "Wondered if you survived."

"And I've always wondered about the man who saved me..."

It's a story I'm sure my kids will never forget.

Survivor and liberator were reunited, in part because I said yes to God. It still makes no sense to me why He chose a mom from Montana to share these men's stories with the world. Why me? I felt unprepared for the task.

One day, I was praying about this very thing. Because of the stories I heard, I could close my eyes and be there. I pictured myself as one of those prisoners. I imagined the pain. I felt the hopelessness. And then I imagined the gates opening and a strong soldier stepping through the gates. My heart rejoiced as I realized that it was my story, after all.

Once chained by sin, I had no hope. I was dying. I was hopeless, and then Jesus opened the gates and led me into freedom— into a life with Him.

Today when I talk about one of "my" veterans, my kids understand. They know the story *behind* the story, which is how I came to write these novels. They know the story *within* the story, which is my salvation and the salvation of all who believe. My kids know that this whole thing wasn't about books and writing. They can tell what God did with my heart.

Sometimes God chooses someone who is in the shape He needs. And sometimes He chooses us and forms us into vessels He can use. That's what He's done for me.

Chapter 22

Pressed In-Between

Yesterday I took my daughter and my grandmother to the shoe store. They both decided they needed new shoes. Leslie had outgrown her old ones, and I think Grandma…well, she just wanted an excuse to get out of the house!

Leslie looked over the aisles and aisles of shoes while I helped Grandma find the perfect pair. When it was time to check out, it turned out that Leslie and Grandma had picked the same shoes—a cute pair of black Roxy shoes with pink shoe-laces. I don't think Leslie would have minded having the same shoes as her great-grandmother. After all, it's not like they hang out in the same places with the same people, but Grandma thought it was just a little weird. After searching a little longer, we found a pair of Dr. Scholl's shoes that actually fit her wide feet better.

What amazed me was not only that my daughter and grandmother had the same taste, but that something so ordinary as shoe shopping could be so delightful to me. To have three women from three generations and sharing the same genes enjoying a few chuckles together—that was something I could have never imagined.

I didn't think about the impact of a family until I became a mom. But the truth is, when I had my son it wasn't just me and him against the world (even though I was ready to do that if needed). Cory was welcomed into a group of people united by history and genes, with lots of struggles and interesting habits. A family that loved him and loved me and reminded me what family is all about.

———

The morning dawned on my first day as a mom. I was too excited to sleep so I snuggled with my baby boy. Cory Joseph had been born at 3:39 a.m., and now that the sun was up, I anticipated the arrival of guests at any minute.

I gazed down at my son's face as he nursed. It amazed me how my body could do that. It had no idea I'd just graduated from high school a few weeks before. Or that I had no job, no savings account, no house of my own, no big plans except for caring for this baby. My body just did its marvelous thing. And Cory didn't seem to mind either. He wasn't worried that I had no 401(k), not even a checking account. I was his mom. That was that.

As I watched Cory, taking in his fragile beauty, immense love overwhelmed me. He'd only been out of my womb a few hours, and I knew I would die for this child.

But I also couldn't help but be a little sad that there wasn't a proud daddy sitting beside me, marveling at this new life. It wasn't just a girlhood fairy tale that took my mind there. Instinctively, I trusted that's how things were supposed to work.

Months earlier I'd been the only single person at Lamaze class and the only mom-to-be there with *her* mom. Even though the nurses and doctors treated me kindly enough, I felt like the odd woman out. As soon as I had my son, I wanted to go home, to return to my safety zone.

The door opened a crack, and my grandparents stepped inside with flowers and a teddy bear. Cory had finished nursing, so I adjusted myself and pulled him out from the blanket.

"There he is!" Grandpa proclaimed.

"Beautiful, just beautiful," my grandma stated with tears in her eyes.

As I looked at her, I didn't know if they were tears of joy over this new family member or tears of heartache that "her little girl" had a baby so young. Or maybe she was thinking back to my mom, who also had me out of wedlock. Or perhaps a combination of all three thoughts.

"It's a nice sunny day outside, not a cloud in the sky," my grandpa said with a nod. To me his words had another meaning: this child was a bright spot in our lives. Things looked positive from here.

As I looked at the faces around me, I knew these people were enough. They were my family. Cory and I belonged.

Belonging to a family means that sometimes you receive love. And sometimes you give it.

John and I had often talked about caring for an aging family member if the need ever arose. My grandparents had lived with us while my grandpa was dying, but we knew that was for a short period of time. After Grandpa's death, my grandmother had moved back to California. But living alone was hard, and after a few years, she was ready to come back. After I received a letter from her and read about her struggles, John and I wanted to open our home to her.

Grandma lived a thousand miles away in the same rural California town where she'd lived her whole life. Yet she found a lot of things challenging, such as maintaining her mobile home, finding help shoveling snow, and stretching the dollars of her meager Social Security check.

Since we knew having an elderly person in our home would result in many changes and sacrifices, we held a family meeting to get our children's input. We shared Grandma's needs and how we'd like to help. Our children agreed we should invite her to live with us. After all, it was what Jesus would do. And the more we talked about it, the more the kids looked forward to having a great-grandma in the house.

Even though we agreed Grandma's living with us was a good thing, all of us struggled with the changes. Grandma went from living alone to being in the midst of constant activity and noise. She'd left behind her church and her friends. Leslie had to share her room with her great-grandmother, so we launched into a construction project to provide Grandma with her own private space. More noise, lots of dust, and lots of mess. Grandma also had special dietary needs, and there was the cost of adding another person to our household.

The most common comment I get when people find out that my grandma lives with us is "Oh, I loved my grandma."

The second is "How do you do it? How do you care for an elderly person *and* kids?"

Most of the time I don't know how to answer this question. It is hard. There are doctor appointments, additional trips to town, and l-o-n-g hours in Wal-Mart, where Grandma spends forty-five minutes looking at all the greeting cards to find "just the right one." But I think we have the better end of the bargain. My children have their great-grandma living with them. How many kids can say that?

As a mom living between two generations, I've learned to see the world from someone else's eyes. Trying to understand my kids is one thing, but really caring about things that matter to a seventy-nine-year-old is tougher. I've learned compassion as I've tried to imagine myself in my grandmother's place. Not only has Grandma gained noise and drama in a house that's always filled with people, she's lost a lot too—her husband, the house she lived in for nearly thirty years, and her home church. She's lost California for Montana, and on a regular basis she receives news that she's lost friends. She's lost the ability to receive visits from other family members. She's lost some of her hearing and a lot of her movement due to bad knees.

There are times it's hard on the kids, too, like on days when Grandma gets upset over a sink full of dishes. (Especially during basketball season when we spend more time on the road than home and we're more concerned about who won or lost than who was supposed to clean the kitchen before we darted out the door.) It's hard during holidays when Grandma's thoughts turn to those she's not celebrating with. And when we're taking another trip to her doctor to figure out a mysterious pain.

Yet those things pale in comparison to what we do have. Grandma's thoughts. Her memories. Her laughter. How many kids get to hear stories about what it was like living in a train boxcar during the Great Depression? (These stories are most likely to pop up when my kids are asking for money or when they throw half their dinner into the trash.)

Some of my favorite things about having Grandma here are practical. I never dreamed I'd have my very own cooking expert and a live-in laundress. But more valuable is the spiritual heritage she has shown my family. Every morning we all hear the beautiful sound of Grandma's prayers and praises coming from her bedroom. It's a heritage that touches my heart...and makes me realize that with this great challenge comes great joy.

The needs of the old and the needs of the young press on me from both sides. Living in a sandwich between two generations pulls, pushes, and squishes me so that I fit. Yet I've discovered that the easier way isn't always the better way. And sometimes what I think will be a big problem—like a family vacation—is the thing that I look back and see as a bonding moment.

Our family had planned for a Florida vacation for five years. Sometimes during bike rides, the kids and I would talk about what theme parks we'd visit, the ocean waves we'd ride, the outrageously expensive park food we'd eat…just because.

Then, when we finally saved enough money, John and I wondered if our dream vacation was still possible. We questioned if Grandma would be physically able to make the trip—or if she'd even enjoy it.

Grandma is sweet and fun—and someone who moves about as fast as a turtle, which she often jokes about. How would she ever handle Walt Disney World?

John and I called a family meeting. We huddled our kids together and discussed our options. Leave Grandma behind? *No.* Take her but leave her in the hotel? *Not fair!* Take her and slow the rest of us down. *Sigh.* It seemed like the right thing to do.

We packed our bags and Grandma's bags too and headed to Florida. It was my grandmother's first big vacation. She'd hardly been out of California her whole life, and never on a big adventure like this.

We hit the beach the first day. The next day would be the theme park we'd all been looking forward to.

Since Grandma had bad knees, we thought we'd take it slow; then we came upon the idea of getting a wheelchair. After waiting in line for one, we finally got her settled.

"I get to push first!" John gripped the handles and moved full speed ahead. Then he picked up speed. Grandma squealed; the rest of us gasped and ran to catch up!

Finally, as we reached the first ride, Grandma burst into laughter. "Who needs a roller coaster?!" she declared.

At the ride, the worker noted our energetic approach. "Are you all together?"

We nodded.

"The wheelchair rider goes to the front of the line…and the rest of the group can go with her."

We felt guilty (and excited) as we passed the others waiting to ride.

After that, the kids took turns pushing. "My turn!"

They also talked Grandma into going on as many rides as possible. After all, she was a free pass to the front!

I'll never forget the laughter of Grandma and Nathan on the ride that blasted us "to outer space." We climbed into the ride with Nathan taking the position of navigator. Grandma was the space commander. The seat rumbled, the ride lifted up, and Grandma worked hard to make sure she did her job—pushing the right buttons, laughing with each shift and roll of our speeding space shuttle.

"You having fun, Grandma?" Nathan asked.

"Oh, yes. I thought I was just taking a trip to Florida. I had no idea we'd go to the moon!"

Of course, the moon was just the first stop on a day filled

with fun. More rides, more shows, and by the end of the day, we felt as if we'd traveled the world.

When the park finally closed and we shuffled outside, Nathan piped up, "That was the best day ever. Grandma, you better live to be a hundred years old because you need to come with me and my kids when we come back!"

Grandma nodded, running her fingers through her ride-blown hair. "You got a date, Nate. You got a date."

Even today, that trip is one of my favorite memories. The sun shone brightly, and I felt God smile.

My grandparents were there for me when I became a mom, and I feel God's pleasure that I'm able to be there for Grandma. It's what family's all about...or so my kids are learning. What I'm learning.

Often God works with us, shaping us with situations and people who we don't think we're prepared to handle. Yet we handle them because He doesn't leave us alone to deal with them. Instead, He holds us and molds us as we hold and care for those who need to feel a loving touch.

Sometimes as God's hands shape my life, they take the form of little fingers and busy hands. But there are other times when the hands that help mold me are knobby and wrinkled and cool to the touch. God, after all, is gentle. Just like Grandma's hands.

Chapter 23

Graduating

I t's been one week since my son's graduation from high school. As I watched him walk down the aisle in cap and gown and mount those steps, I realized it was the second time he'd been on stage during a high school graduation ceremony.

The first time, Cory was inside me. It was three weeks before I was due to deliver, and it took every ounce of guts to put on my graduation robe, face the stares of almost everyone I knew in our town of three thousand, and mount those steps.

Until a month before that day, I had no intention of graduating. I'd dropped out of high school six months earlier because I was too embarrassed to go to school pregnant. But since I'd earned the credits I needed at a community school, the principal gave me the opportunity to graduate with my class…if I wanted to. Three factors guided my decision.

1. I had gone to school since kindergarten with most of the other thirty-six people graduating, and I couldn't imagine not attending and watching them graduate.

2. I didn't want to sit in the audience and not be with them on stage. I knew everyone would see me— and gawk at me—whether I was on stage or in the crowd. A hugely pregnant seventeen-year-old is hard to miss.

3. Graduating with my class was one of my first steps toward redeeming myself after my mistakes. It was a way to prove to everyone, mostly myself, that I could have a good future.

Cory's graduation, of course, was far different. While the number of students was about the same, the ceremony centered on God and family and how good character leads to good futures. And as homeschooling parents, we were the ones privileged to present the diplomas to our kids, which only makes sense since we were the teachers, the principals, and the guidance counselors from kindergarten through twelfth grade. (Hey, after all our work, we wanted five minutes of recognition too!)

The ceremony went smoothly, just as planned. The only thing I didn't expect was my unpreparedness for my son's education to be over. I wanted to yell, "Hold on. Wait a minute. Stop that *Pomp and Circumstance*. Can we try this again next year? Please, halt the ceremony, people. Let's ditch the gown.

"After all, we never did finish that reading of *Huckleberry Finn* we started in eighth grade, and I don't think he's mastered algebra, not to mention that his spelling *still* needs work. And I wanted to somehow squeeze in a trip to Washington DC before this day came. That hasn't happened, so maybe we can give it another year and see if I can complete those items still on my list."

Of course, I didn't say those things. Instead, I congratulated Cory on a job well done, even though I didn't feel done myself. Maybe I'll never feel done.

Did I do enough right things to make up for all the good intentions I never got around to?

Have I prepared him for life?

Did I do a good enough job pointing Cory to eternity?

Questions like these knotted together like two dozen hot-pink jump ropes jumbled in my gut. Nineteen years ago, my mind was filled with questions about my future. Now, my mind is filled with questions about *my son's* future. And his, it seems, matters more.

Maybe it matters more because I've spent the last eighteen years guiding and training and praying for Cory's adulthood. I didn't spend nearly that much time thinking about my future. My life, circumstances, pregnancy, and finishing my senior year by doing schoolwork on my parents' living room couch just sort of happened.

As I was graduating into adulthood, I was already stepping into parenting. Walking across the stage with a baby growing inside me was like launching into a never-ending series of end-of-the-year finals. Pregnancy, birth, sleeping all night, potty training, manner training, truth telling, worldview understanding.

The only problem is I didn't know how final those milestones were, until they were past.

———

I can't help but think of all those older women who stopped me in the grocery store when my kids were little and told me, "Enjoy this time; they grow so fast."

Every time they'd say it, I'd think: *Enjoy this time?! Are you nuts? I haven't peed without someone pounding on the bathroom door or showered alone or read two pages of a novel uninterrupted for three months. I'm supposed to enjoy this?*

Yet they were right. The time did go fast. Way too fast.

Even now, I'm chuckling over the idea that I'm writing about my child's graduation. I'm only thirty-six years old, for goodness' sake! Many of my former classmates haven't even started their families yet. The only thing that consoles me and makes me feel like I'm not *that* old is that I have two more kids, who are still at home and still very much in need of training and schooling and guidance, and, I hope, other children (through adoption) who haven't joined our family yet.

How different is my state of mind at this graduation than at the previous one. When I first found out I was pregnant with Cory, I hoped it wasn't true. I was scared about what my life would become. But you know what? My fears were unfounded. I had thought my choices had destroyed my life, but God took my repentance over my sin and used it to form me into a woman who could hope. Who could dream of, strive for, a good future. As I thought of taking care of someone other than myself, I got serious about making good choices, beginning with the decision to give my life to Christ.

For many years before that decision, I'd believed *in* God. I'd even attended church when I was a child. Only when I came to the end of myself and was completely scared and confused and overwhelmed did I turn *to* Him. My life had become a soap opera, yet the drama wasn't nearly as exciting. In the end I couldn't deal with what life had become, and I was pretty much holed up in my room.

Then I thought of Jesus…and all those Bible stories I'd heard as a kid…and I wrapped my arms around my stomach and prayed. *God, I've screwed up big time, but if you can do something better with my life, please do.*

He *has* done better.

He gave me hope and peace and joy, which are some of the best attributes a mom can have. He also connected me with a body of people who didn't just gawk at me but opened their arms to me in love. He shaped and molded me into the type of person who could raise kids to love God and put Him first in their lives.

I thought about all of this in the weeks preceding Cory's graduation. And I realized that in most stages of our lives—and of our children's lives—we will never be ready. Each new step brings new trials, and there will always be things we wish we had done differently and better.

I wasn't ready when Cory headed off to preschool or when he drove away alone in his car for the first time. I wasn't ready when Leslie headed off to her first prom, dressed up like a storybook princess. I wasn't ready for Nathan's first sleepover or first children's camp far from home. And actually, I believe that feeling unsure and unprepared is a good place to be. It makes us learn about trust. It makes us turn to God.

In fact, as our children grow, we can view each new step as a step closer to our heavenly Father, as we turn to Him for help, guidance, and strength in this new stage of life.

As James wrote about in his letter to fellow believers, it's the testing of our faith that develops perseverance. (And what can test us more than our kids? Or our lack of readiness to deal with our kids!) It's through persevering, through the training and the shaping and the molding of our children, that God trains and shapes and molds *us*—making us mature and complete.

Some people may wrongly assume that raising our kids is all about the kids growing up. It's not. It's about us using these challenging times to grow up ourselves. As we watch our kids grow into the people God designed them to be, we are also participating in our own transformation. God uses parenting to shape and mold us. The woman who walked across the stage for her son's graduation is different than the pregnant young woman who walked across for her own. And Cory's been one of the factors for her—my—growth.

I've come to see each new step taken by one of my children as a graduation of my own.

When Leslie stayed the first time at a friend's house without crying or feeling frightened or calling to be picked up during the night, I felt proud. She had learned trust and confidence. She had learned that God is always with her. She had realized that she could live apart from me. (A concept I'd questioned for many years as she clung to my leg at every social event.)

When Nathan went on his first missions trip and volunteered at a soup kitchen, I realized that he knew the importance of serving others and giving to those in need.

When Cory produced his own video series for youth group, I worried he wouldn't be able to write, shoot, and produce what he'd promised. Yet Cory stuck to what he promised to do, giving up fun summer outings to complete his work. Wow, what a big leap of maturity from the high schooler I used to have to nag to get his homework done.

Seeing all of the ways they've outgrown their need for my constant presence or nagging persistence, I don't a need cap and gown and tassel to tell me I've also taken a new step as a mom. Instead, I feel it inside.

———

These days the times I play with play dough are few and far between, yet it's easy to remember the lesson. During the years of motherhood, there were times I believed I'd never get the crumbs out. There were other times it hurt so much as God pulled and tugged me into shape. But today, if I picture myself in His hands, I can see I'm much more pliable. I'm also closer to the image God pictured in His mind from creation—a picture that closely resembled Christ. No, I haven't arrived, but I'm closer. Closer to God, closer to my children, closer to understanding that every part of our journey is necessary in the molding, even those years when we struggle with spit-up and tummy aches and tantrums. Especially those years.

God molded me through motherhood because I was willing to place myself in His hands. I was needy and He was there to help.

And now that my kids are older, the molding hasn't stopped. It's different and it's welcomed, because I now realize more than ever that the best place to be is plopped into God's hands.

Yes, that's the very best place to be. Ever. Always.

Acknowledgments

For every book I write, I struggle with who to thank—not because there isn't anyone, but because there are so many.

I am especially grateful to those who live with me (John, Cory, Leslie, Nathan, Grandma, and Andrea) and those in my life (church friends, community friends, writer friends, online friends). Thank you, each one!

I always thank my agent, Janet Grant, because she's the most amazing agent ever. And my assistant, Amy Lathrop, because she manages my life and I'd be a big mess without her. I also always thank my mom, dad, and other family members, because they love me, mess and all.

For this book a few people get *mucho* credit. Liz Heaney and Alice Crider, two amazing editors who kept urging me to "dig deeper." Thank you for helping me make sense of my stories and share them in a way that makes sense to the world.

Most of all, thanks to David Kopp who saw this book from the beginning even better than I could. The expression "thanks for believing in me" might be common, but the emotions that come with it are rare. You didn't let me off easy, Dave, but I'm growing into the writer you recognized deep within. Thank you.

Wanna Do it Right Without the eXPERT ADVICE?

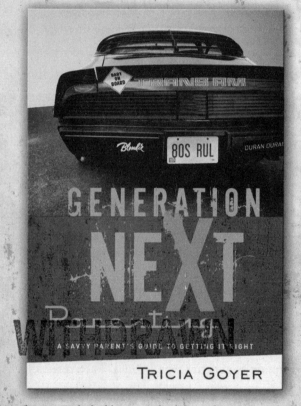

BABY ON BOARD

TRANS AM

Blondie 80S RUL DURAN DURAN

GENERATION
NeXt
Parenting
WITHDRAWN

A SAVVY PARENT'S GUIDE TO GETTING IT RIGHT

TRICIA GOYER

Looking for practical, doable tips and guidance for raising today's kids?
Want to help them love God and be all that they can be (even if they don't
join the Army)? Extensive research, input from hundreds of Gen X moms
and dads, and a variety of Scripture references will help you navigate even
the toughest parenting dilemmas.

www.triciagoyer.com